"Every child struggles to find his or her way in life, but for children dealing with a disability, finding the way can seem filled with dead ends. How do we shepherd a child through those difficult seasons? In *Caring for the Souls of Children*, you will find a rich resource of wise insights, seasoned advice, and solid biblical guidance to help children view their limitations from God's point of view. I give this much-needed book a double thumbs-up!"

Joni Eareckson Tada, Founder and CEO, Joni and Friends International Disability Center

"Some books overpromise, but not this one. On all the most pressing issues in counseling (and parenting!) children, *Caring for the Souls of Children* delivers with grace and wisdom. I highly recommend this resource."

J. Alasdair Groves, Executive Director, Christian Counseling and Educational Foundation (CCEF)

"This wonderful book about counseling children (and teens) fills an important gap in biblical counseling resources. We are reminded that children experience the same kinds of problems and fears that adults do and thus need our help. This book will be of great practical use as the authors present many realistic counseling situations in which they walk the reader through a wise, compassionate, and biblical way to help hurting children. This resource will be a of great help to pastors and counselors who work with children and teens. I plan to highly recommend it to all of my students."

Jim Newheiser, Director of the Christian Counseling Program and Associate Professor of Pastoral Theology, Reformed Theological Seminary; Executive Director, The Institute for Biblical Counseling and Discipleship (IBCD)

"As a longtime biblical counseling pastor and now professor, I have waited over thirty years for a book like this! Amy Baker and her team provide a one-stop shop of readable, gospel-centered, biblically-driven strategies to help counselors and caring adults minister to kids facing all sorts of struggles. Children need Jesus; this book helps us bring him to them."

Robert D. Jones, The Southern Baptist Theological Seminary; author of *Pursuing Peace* and *Anger: Calming Your Heart*

"If you work with children in any capacity, you need *Caring for the Souls of Children*. This counseling manual is a rich, robust resource addressing the vast array of issues related to child soul care. It provides introduction to methodology and theory, addresses common but often overlooked aspects of counseling children, and delves into the darkest challenges a counselor will face with instruction for counseling topics like self-harm, trauma, and post-suicide counseling."

Curtis Solomon, Executive Director of the Biblical Counseling Coalition

"Dr. Amy Baker and her team of writers have greatly served the church of Jesus Christ by assembling this important book. The chapters are both practical and theologically robust. Surely the Lord is pleased when counselors give special care to ministering to children. These truths will also be helpful to parents, teachers, and children's ministry leaders."

Steve Viars, Senior Pastor, Faith Church, Lafayette, IN; author of *Loving Your Community*

"Whether to counsel children and how to counsel children are some of the most common questions within the biblical counseling movement, yet there have been few resources available on this topic. Thankfully, a team of well-qualified counselors and trusted authors have worked together to fill a gap in the biblical counseling literature. If you counsel and you have struggled knowing how to serve the children in your community, then this resource is a must-read."

Rob Green, Pastor of Counseling and Seminary Ministries, Faith Church, Lafayette, IN; author of *Tying the Knot* and *Tying Their Shoes*

CARING FOR THE SOULS OF CHILDREN

. . . .

CARING FOR THE SOULS OF CHILDREN

. . . .

A BIBLICAL COUNSELOR'S MANUAL

. . . .

AMY BAKER, EDITOR

New Growth Press

newgrowthpress.com

New Growth Press, Greensboro, NC 27404
newgrowthpress.com
Chapters copyrighted © 2020 by named author; Ch. 12 Copyright © 2020 by
Harvest USA; Chs. 14 & 15 © 2020 by Joni and Friends

Cover Design: Faceout Books, faceoutstudio.com
Interior Design and Typesetting: Gretchen Logterman

ISBN: 978-1-64507-063-4 (Print)
ISBN: 978-1-64507-064-1 (eBook)

Library of Congress Cataloging-in-Publication Data on file
Identifiers: LCCN 2020015693 (print) | LCCN 2020015694 (ebook)

Printed in the United States of America

27 26 25 24 23 22 21 20   2 3 4 5 6

CONTENTS

Part 1

Foundation and Methodological Issues

CHAPTER 1

The Soul of a Child:
An Introduction to Counseling Children

AMY BAKER

The parents of eleven-year-old Maya[1] were concerned because Maya seemed to be withdrawing from friends and family. She no longer asked to spend time with her friends, and at home she had begun isolating herself in her room. Although she had been a good student in the past, now she didn't complete her homework unless compelled by her parents, and she no longer seemed to care about her grades. Fights with her two older sisters were becoming increasingly common, and she had begun lying to her parents.

Maya's brother was killed in a car accident when he was six years old and Maya was seven. A drunk driver had swerved off the street and hit the boy in the family's front yard, killing him instantly. It took a while, but over time it appeared everyone in the family accepted what had happened and gradually moved on with life—until Maya began to visibly disengage from everything that had been important to her.

Now Maya's parents feel stuck. They don't feel like they can reach her. They have brought their daughter to biblical counseling in hopes that someone outside the family will be able to connect with Maya. Maya and her family became regular church attenders within the last two years, and Maya made a profession of faith some time ago. While Maya was a bit nervous about counseling, she was not completely resistant to the idea of talking with someone.

It was my privilege to meet with Maya, while another counselor worked with Maya's parents. As I met with this precious child, I was struck anew with the profound thoughts and questions in an eleven-year-old's soul. We often think children need a completely different approach to counseling than adults. It is certainly true that we need to tailor interactions with them to the development and understanding of the child; we won't talk with and interact with a child the same way we would with an adult. But despite the differences in how we communicate and draw a child out, my observations after years of working with children demonstrate:

- Children struggle with the *same* desires adults struggle with.
- They are lured by the *same* lies adults fall prey to.
- They find hope in the *same* source adults find hope—in our Lord and Savior.

For children, the struggles, desires, and hopes are no different than for those of us who are adults. Therefore, the counsel we provide for them should lead them to the same place—the good news of Jesus Christ.

Children, like adults, wrestle with profound thoughts and questions and need to see how the gospel connects to them in their current struggles. At one point in our counseling, I asked Maya to draw a picture for me of her relationship with God. The picture she drew was gut-wrenching.

Her picture had four frames.

- In frame one, she depicted herself kneeling by her bed to pray to God.
- In frame two, she showed God responding to her prayer by saying, "Hmm . . . her. Her prayers don't matter."
- In frame three, she depicted herself searching for answers by reading the Bible, questioning why she couldn't find answers.
- In her final frame, she drew God responding to her Bible study by asking, "Why should I give her answers?!"

As we discussed this, Maya told me she didn't believe God responded to everyone this way, just her. She was convinced she was different. Maya shared that she didn't think she was precious to God. Maya also said that she didn't think God always means what he says in the Bible.

I concluded from these remarks that it would be fruitless to immediately direct Maya to passages that show the depth of God's love for her. I felt certain that Maya would be convinced these passages might be true for everyone else, but not for her.

The Help We Need Is the Help Children Need

Along with other resources, I decided to have Maya look at the book of Job with me. Even as I directed her to Job 1, I was internally asking myself if I was being unwise. Job is not the easiest book in the Bible to digest, and here I was asking an eleven-year-old girl to study it.

Nevertheless, I went ahead and told her the story of Job—a man who was suffering and didn't understand what God was doing. As we dug deeper, it became apparent this was exactly the truth Maya needed to hear as she wrestled with the tragedy of her brother's death.

As counselors, we need to be reminded that the answers from Scripture are not too hard for children to grasp.

After looking at Job 1, Maya initially observed that, like Job, God was letting Satan into her life, but, unlike Job, she was not keeping faith. Maya also shared that Job got answers, but she didn't get answers.

Then we looked at Job 3, where Job questions what God is doing. We talked together about how Job didn't understand God or what he was doing.

Over the next few sessions, we continued to look at Job. We spent time in Job 9 and 10, looking at some of the conclusions Job drew about God, about life, and about himself.

- Job 9:14–20—God won't answer my questions.
- Job 9:21—I despise my life.
- Job 9:22—There is no difference in how God treats the wicked or the blameless.
- Job 9:23—God mocks the despair of innocent people.
- Job 9:25–28—Even if I decide I'll act like I'm happy, God will still be against me.
- Job 9:29—Since God has already decided I'm guilty, what's the use of trying?
- Job 9:30–31—Even if I tried to clean myself up, God would just make me dirty again.

- Job 9:32–35—If I could go to court and get an impartial judge, the judge would tell God I'm good.
- Job 10:1—I loathe my life.

I asked this eleven-year-old to identify where she had similar questions and thoughts. To my surprise, Maya was able to reframe each of Job's responses to a similar struggle in her own soul. Maya identified similar thoughts to all these things.

Like adults, children need to wrestle with sin and suffering and be led to see a sovereign, merciful God at work.
Eventually we moved to the end of Job and God's response to him. I observed that God didn't answer Job's questions; rather, God revealed himself. Following this, we looked at Job's response:

> Then Job replied to the LORD:
> "I know that you can do all things;
> no purpose of yours can be thwarted.
> You asked, 'Who is this that obscures my plans without knowledge?'
> Surely I spoke of things I did not understand,
> things too wonderful for me to know. (Job 42:1–3 NIV)

I paraphrased Job's response in the following way: "God is at work doing things far more wonderful than I can understand or imagine. I need to trust him." As part of her homework, I asked Maya to write this on a card and reflect on this response several times each day.

When Maya came back the following week, she had done an excellent job of thinking about Job's response, and she had made some connections between Job's response to her response and her life. This gave her some hope. When I asked Maya to continue to reflect on this paraphrase for another week, she confided that she intended to write it out on another card and put the first card on the wall by her bed.

This was not the sum of our counseling. We also looked at Christ, who was dearly loved by his Father yet cried in agony on the cross, "Why have you forsaken me?" Our discussion of Job was a tiny snippet in a process that would take months to complete. And even when we stopped meeting, the book wasn't closed. Maya, like all of us, is a work in progress. God in his kindness guides us in our walk with him, step-by-step. Maya will face new questions as she gets older, just as all of us find we need to ask for more and more wisdom.

But for eleven-year-old Maya, the struggles, the desires, and the hope were no different than for those of us who are adults. That's the core thesis of this book, and that's the reason we boldly proclaim that Christ is our Light and God's Word is sufficient for all counseling, regardless of age group.

The Core of Counseling Children

Throughout this book, you'll hear from a number of counselors who are convinced of the same premise—the struggles, the desires, and the source of hope for children are no different than the struggles, desires, and source of hope for adults. Again, while taking into account the developmental level of a child and the best way to convey this truth, we want to encourage counselors and parents to boldly trust in the sufficiency of God and his Word to help struggling children. (See chapter 3, Counseling Children of Different Age Groups, for a discussion of taking into account children's age and stage of development.)

From this starting place, we want to lovingly help the children we counsel become individuals who find God to be exceedingly magnificent, trustworthy, and good. Then as a result, they can live with the desire to be a more and more accurate image of his beauty by loving him and others, using the Word of God to teach them (as it does us) how to do this.

The specific presenting problem that prompts children to come to counseling is merely the laboratory set up by God to facilitate this process. These individualized "labs" may seem to have features constructed from nature (the child's biology, e.g., autism, learning disabilities) or from nurture (the child's environment, e.g., abuse, divorce), but it would be a mistake to believe these are controlling features. Both nature and nurture are under the hand of the all-wise Creator, who provides everything needed for life in his Word—for with him is the fountain of life (Psalm 36:9).

So, as we prepare to meet with children, we know we will talk about suffering, we will talk about sin, but our foremost topic will be our Savior because in his light, we see light (Psalm 36:9). In Part Two of this book, we'll discuss how you might do this in a variety of areas where children struggle.

It saddens us to think that those who want to come alongside children would mistakenly believe children somehow need different answers to life's problems than adults need. Christ is our Light! He is *the* way, *the* truth, and *the* life. There is not a separate way for children that differs in essence from the way for adults. Christ is the way.

Decisions on Meeting with a Child Individually

It might surprise you to learn that in a book on counseling children, we would not normally suggest counseling the child as the first option. We would normally encourage counseling for the parents—to equip them to counsel their child. Here's why: We want to do everything we can to help parents with their children. God has entrusted these precious souls to parents, and God gives the parents preferential status in bringing these children up (status he has not given to the schools, the government, the church, youth workers, or biblical counselors). God has conferred to parents the primary oversight—and resulting blessing—of these children. So, as counselors, we want to view it as our first responsibility to equip the parents to carry out this privileged commission from God. The implication of this is that whenever possible, we want to meet first with the parents to equip them to help their child. At times, this may be all that is needed.

However, we believe it's possible for helpers to become unbalanced in this position, to the point where children in need are neglected. There are many reasons why directly counseling children can be important. For example, we would certainly want to consider direct counseling for the child in the following situations:

- When the parents need significant help with their own issues before being equipped to help their child, and we want the child to get immediate help
- When the parent-child relationship is so poor that the child will no longer respond to the parent
- When a judge orders counseling specifically and directly for child

- When a child won't open up in front of a parent (perhaps due to abuse, anger, or fear)
- When parents have no interest in following God but are willing to allow their child to get biblical counseling
- When a young teen has started asking his or her youth pastor or teacher questions about life, and the parents see this as a positive opportunity to allow the child to learn to seek wise counsel from mature believers

In situations where we can best serve the family and the child by meeting with the child directly, our goal would usually be to have at least one parent present as we work with the child. This is what I was able to do with Maya. Maya's parents were deeply concerned about Maya but felt out of their depth in handling the pressing issues they were observing in her life. I wanted her parents to know what Maya and I were discussing so they could follow up and gain confidence in their discussions with Maya.

So, while we may first investigate equipping the parents, there will be times we want to meet with the parents and the child together, and other times when we will meet with the child alone.

Progressive Growth

If asked, I believe many of us might report that we feel inadequate when it comes to counseling children. Years ago, when I began to work at a Baptist Children's Home (BCH), I was given the responsibility of meeting as counselor and social worker with some children in the care of BCH. I felt way out of my league in this role. What should I say? What should I do?

When I entered the counseling room with these children, I needed help from the same gospel I hoped to unpack for them. Both the children and I entered the meeting in the care of the One who holds the power of the universe in his hands and who would never use that power to do evil against us. Instead, he was willing to use our very weaknesses and vulnerability as a conduit for pouring out his own grace and power in our lives.

Both these children and I started from the same page— we were loved by a Redeemer who would never abandon us in the middle of a session. Instead, he would work all things together to transform us into his image, the image of One who loved so completely that he would withhold nothing good but *would* powerfully and kindly withhold anything which would not be good (Romans 8:28–32).

I made a lot of missteps in my time with those children. But, although I was a flawed representative, God also mercifully allowed me to be his servant ambassador:

- To children who had been abused
- To children facing the death of a parent
- To children who were angry and rebellious
- To children who would never be reunited with their parents
- To children who would be reunited with their parents but would return to homes full of conflict and hate

While I was tempted to despair over my inadequacies, God never wavered in his promise that he would use even my missteps for his own good purposes (Romans 8:28–29; see also Isaiah 46:3–4, 8–13). He will do the same for you.

We hope that the chapters that follow will help you be better equipped for the opportunities God entrusts to you in counseling children. We want to encourage you not to wait until you feel completely confident before you minister to hurting children, but to let your sense of inadequacy push you to deeper dependence on the Lord as you strive to be his faithful messenger of hope. Let me encourage you with this modified quote from Joe Thorn, which he wrote in a blog about praying for your pastor,[2] but which I believe applies equally to those who want to counsel children:

> Counselors often struggle with feelings of failure after they step away from the counseling room. Counseling days can be times of doubt and frustration for many counselors. Pray that you would be so satisfied with what you have in Christ that even if you lost your way while counseling you would remain confident that Christ has neither lost you nor his word. Ask God to give you such confidence in the Spirit's power and the Scripture's sufficiency that should your counseling fail to live up to your standards, your hope remains steadfast for God can use any person's counseling, no matter how deficient, as long as she or he gives the people the word. Pray that you would have the mindset that "success" is simply faithfulness to God, and fruitfulness determined by God.

CHAPTER 2
METHODOLOGY: KEY ELEMENTS IN COUNSELING CHILDREN

AMY BAKER

You've been asked by your senior pastor to counsel an eight-year-old child. You don't usually directly counsel children this young; you usually counsel parents and equip them to come alongside their young children to provide the hope and help the child needs.

However, in this situation, based on other conversations with the parents, your pastor has concluded that offering to counsel the parents about their child's struggles will simply result in the parents searching out a counseling agency that will work directly with their child. The parents are very willing to be involved as participants in counseling, but they would also like their eight-year-old daughter Kylee to be an active participant.

You are aware of the amazing gospel opportunity present in this situation, but you feel way out of your league. Where do you start?

In this chapter we're going to cover important counseling components for working with children. These key elements will give you principles for structuring your counseling sessions with children. Consider them a backbone to use for support as you proceed. It may or may not surprise you to learn this backbone is basically the same as what we would use for counseling adults.

The means of hope and salvation for a child are the same as for an adult—Jesus Christ. In light of this core reality, our fundamental message in counseling doesn't change when we address children. The principal difference between counseling a child versus an adult is making sure our approach and language are accessible and easily digestible by a child.

You may find that your counseling can be greatly enhanced if you have targeted resources to help you connect with the child in front of you. Entire psychological therapies have been built around using resources and techniques that facilitate connecting with children—play therapy, art therapy, and more. Researchers in the fields of psychology, social work, and counseling have worked hard to identify helpful ways to relate with children, encourage their involvement with the counseling process, gather data, and give instruction. If you're going to counsel children regularly, you may want to invest in some of these tools to help facilitate your counseling.[1] This may be an excellent way to show love to a struggling child.

You needn't be intimidated about the prospect of counseling a child. As you prayerfully approach building a connection with a young person and looking for inroads to share truth, keep in mind the core theme of your counseling is not dependent on these tools, nor dependent upon you feeling like an expert. Over time you may develop more helpful tools to aid you, but your message will be unchanging. So, while you may invest in action figures, children's games, and markers and crayons, these are just helpful tools to enhance your basic message.

Tools may be helpful, but they will not be the primary focus in this book. Our primary focus is to equip you to use the Word of God to help children see what an exceedingly magnificent, trustworthy, and good God we have and assist them to be more and more accurate images of God's beauty by loving him and others.

That said, let's consider seven structural components for counseling that can be a backbone for your counseling. These key elements are 1) show love and begin to build a relationship, 2) gather relevant data, 3) evaluate the problem biblically, 4) share biblical hope, 5) provide biblical instruction, 6) assign practical homework, and 7) involve the parents.

Show Love and Begin to Build a Relationship

Someone has said that people don't care how much you know until they know how much you care. While this observation isn't universally true, I think most of us find that we take instruction from and respond better to people we believe care about us.

Look for opportunities to show that you want to build a relationship with the child even before you get to the counseling office. For example, when you first meet eight-year-old Kylee, you may want to kneel down to introduce yourself so you are looking at Kylee at her eye level as you say hello. Otherwise, you may tower over her and seem intimidating (kneeling, rather than bending, makes one less imposing).

For children (as with many adults), walking into unknown situations can produce anxiety. When children come for counseling, they may have no idea what to expect. They may have questions about counseling that no one has answered.

Questions children may have about counseling include:

- What is counseling, and why do I have to go there?
- Did I do something wrong? Am I being punished?
- Is something wrong with me?
- Do Mom and Dad think something is wrong with me? Do they love me?
- Will my friends think something is wrong with me? Will they make fun of me if they find out?
- Will it hurt? Is it like going to the doctor?
- How long does it take? When will I get to leave?
- If I don't like it, will I have to go back?
- What am I supposed to say and do? What if I say something wrong?
- Should I tell bad things about my family?
- Will the counselor tell anyone what I say?[2]

Show love to the children by explaining what will happen in counseling and answering their questions. You might begin with an explanation like this: "Your parents wanted me to meet with you because they think you are going through some hard things right now. They want to be sure you have someone you can talk to who will listen to you and work hard to understand what is happening. It's my job to listen, to work hard to understand, and then to help you learn what to do about these hard things. Because I'm a biblical counselor, that means I'm going to depend on God and the Bible for answers."

As you seek to show love and build a relationship with children you counsel, remember you are asking them to communicate some of the most difficult and troubling aspects of their lives to you. It may be that the child has been abused, and describing what occurred can bring feelings of great shame. It may be that the child's parents are divorcing, and the child fears that if she does anything wrong, her remaining parent will leave. It may be that that the child is wrestling with his sexual identity and believes that if he tells you, you'll condemn him.

As you seek to build a relationship, try to understand what it would be like to live in their world. See the children as individuals who suffer and need your compassion.

Whatever issue has prompted the need for counsel, it will be deeply personal to this precious soul who now sits in your office. Few of us feel ready to share our vulnerabilities with a stranger, so we as counselors should proceed slowly and thoughtfully.

Gather Relevant Data

Gathering relevant data means asking appropriate questions and listening carefully to understand what is happening in the child's life and heart. Often data gathering begins before a first meeting. At our counseling center, we ask the parents (and the child, if possible) to give us some preliminary data. We ask for written answers to the following questions.

- What is the main problem, as you see it? What brings you here?
- What have you done about it?
- What can we do? What expectations do you have in coming here?
- As you see yourself, what kind of person are you?
- Is there any other information we should know?

Kylee's parents gave the following answers to these questions:

- Kylee has been showing increasing anger toward her four-year-old brother. Recently she threw a glass at him, which could have caused serious injury if her aim had been better.
- We have tried to get Kylee to be kind to her brother. We have given her stickers to be nice and given her room time when she is mean.
- We need someone to help Kylee learn to control her anger.
- Kylee is usually kind and caring. She is well liked at school and gets good grades.
- We want Kylee to be able to meet with the counselor by herself if that would be helpful to her. We want to do whatever we can to help our daughter.

Even if I am aware of how the child is struggling prior to our first meeting, I don't generally start out talking about the hard part of the child's life. In my counseling, I usually try to begin with easier questions (some of which I'll already know the answer to based on intake forms). I like to learn where the child lives, who lives with her (and the relationships of each of these individuals to the child—mother, stepdad, biological brother, stepsister, etc.), how old her siblings are, whether she has pets, what grade she is in, where she goes to school, if she is a good student, what she likes best about school, what she likes least about school, or what she likes to do when she's not in school.

Occasionally I may give bits of information about myself. For example, "You like math? Math was always hard for me." Or, "I was the middle kid in my family too." Sharing information is how relationships are built, and I want to make it apparent that I want to develop a relationship.

If you are going to counsel children regularly, you may find it helpful to invest in some ice breakers—like board games—to help you learn about the child while doing something they enjoy. This has the benefit of easing the tension for scared or nervous children by allowing them to answer while doing something like playing a game—rather than looking directly at a stranger who is asking questions.

As the children begin to feel more at ease with you and the counseling setting, you may begin to transition into questions that give you a better understanding of the hard parts in their lives. With Kylee, you may want to find out how she feels about coming to counseling. Is she scared about meeting with you? Is she mad because she has to come? Why did her parents think it was important for her to meet with a counselor? Does Kylee agree? What is Kylee's relationship like with her little brother? Is her brother ever a pain? What does she do when her brother is a pain? What is her understanding of God's role in her relationships?

Not all children are skilled in verbally describing where they are struggling. It may be tempting in such situations to make assumptions about the effect of the children's circumstances on them. While these assumptions may often be accurate, you'll probably find it's much better to learn from the children themselves. Look for other ways to learn answers to the questions you have. Sometimes you can do this by asking questions in a different way.

Another way to gather data is to ask the child to draw a picture. For example, you might ask a child to draw a picture of the best part of their lives and a picture of the hardest part of their lives. Once they have drawn the picture, you can ask them to explain it. This can sometimes be an effective way of gathering relevant data.

Sometimes children find it helpful to have a parent describe what is happening. I find this helpful as well. Involving the parents when I'm gathering data often gives me a richer description of the problem. In doing this, I want to make sure that I am still engaging the child. So, after hearing from the parent, I may ask the child what she thought about what her parent just told me. I may ask the child to tell me other details the parent didn't think to tell me, and rather than directing follow-up questions toward the parent, I will ask the child follow-up questions.

Counseling should involve lots of interaction, asking appropriate questions and listening carefully to understand what is happening in the child's life. This doesn't come naturally for most of us. Learning to ask good questions is a skill that is developed and honed by practice over time. If you find yourself doing most of the talking, this may mean you have morphed into a Sunday school teacher rather than a counselor. Instead of preparing a lesson in advance, you may find it more helpful to make a robust list of questions. These questions will help you learn about the child and encourage the child to think about the important issues of life.

Here are some questions that may serve as a springboard to gather relevant data. These are just to help you prime the pump; they're not meant to be a checklist for a meeting with a child.

- Who is your favorite person on earth? Why? What kinds of things do you do together?

- Who is the hardest person in your life to be around? What do you do when that person is around?
- Tell me how many kids are buying/using drugs at your school? Has anyone ever shared their drugs with you? What happened?
- Are there a lot of gangs at your school? Are your friends in gangs?
- Who are the most popular kids at your school? Are you one of the popular kids?
- Do you think you're good-looking/smart/funny/athletic?
- How many kids in your class do you think have had sex? What do you think of that?
- How many transgender kids do you know? Gay kids?
- If you were to get a tattoo, where would you put it and what would it be?
- Do you have a boyfriend/girlfriend? How long have you been together? Does your boyfriend/girlfriend want to have sex with you? Do you want to have sex?
- Do people ask you what you want to be when you grow up? What do you tell them?
- If you go to church, do you like to go? Why or why not?
- Would you say you are a person who is full of hope?
- Do people ever make fun of you?
- Who are the biggest bullies in your class? Do they bully you? How do you handle that? What do you do to protect yourself from being bullied?
- Do you think God would ever be your friend? What would it be like to have God as your friend?
- What are the best and worst things that have ever happened to you?

- What is the worst thing that ever happened in your family?
- When do your parents tell you "no" the most frequently?
- Do you ever ask God for help when things are hard? If you have asked God for help, what happened? If you haven't asked God for help, how do you think God would have responded if you had asked him for help?
- If your life doesn't turn out the way you want, what will you do?

Evaluate the Problem Biblically

As I begin to get to know the child, my job will be to interpret what I'm learning using the lens of the Word of God. I want to learn what is going on in the child's heart because Proverbs 4:23 reminds us that the heart is the wellspring of our life— it's our control center.

Initially the child may see the problem only as something outside of her. For example, you may learn from Kylee that her four-year-old brother has been getting into her stuff—breaking things and making a mess. The most recent conflict occurred after he ruined her favorite shoes. When you ask how she responded to her brother's actions, she may tell you that she told her parents about the problem and asked him to stop. As you ask more questions, you may learn that Kylee also began hitting her brother, and after the last incident, she threw a glass at him. Clearly, her aggression toward him has been escalating. According to Kylee, the problem is her brother. For Kylee, as with others you may counsel, the solution seems to be looking for ways to remove or ameliorate the external pressures. Kylee's solution to the problem requires finding ways to prevent her brother from getting into her stuff.

However, this would not be a thoroughly biblical evaluation of the problem. While it is entirely appropriate to learn what the external pressures are and to suggest ways to remove or lessen the impact of these pressures, we are not providing biblical counseling if this is the sum of our advice.

Consider the popular illustration of squeezing a plastic bottle of water until the liquid inside spills out. If we look at the spill and ask, why is there a puddle of water on the floor? the answer is often, because we squeezed the bottle. However, we must also consider that the reason there is water on the floor is because there was water inside the bottle. There is not Mountain Dew on the floor; there is not milk on the floor. There is water. What is on the floor can only be there because that's what was originally in the bottle.

In this illustration, squeezing the bottle represents pressure from the child's circumstances and environment. As pressure is put on the child by external factors, what is in the heart of the child comes spilling out. The contents of the heart are not changed by the pressure, the pressure simply brings the heart to the surface so that it can be seen. If the heart is full of fear and anger, pressure will bring out fear and anger.

As biblical counselors we want to skillfully gather relevant data so we can accurately evaluate what is going on in the heart. Evaluating the problem biblically puts us in a stronger position to offer God's promises of comfort, freedom from guilt, forgiveness, release from shame, peace that transcends all understanding, and, most importantly, a Savior, King, and Redeemer.

In Kylee's situation, the external pressure of her four-year-old brother messing with her stuff has brought to the surface anger and aggression. What desires, motives, and fears are causing aggression to come spilling out? James asks, "What causes fights and quarrels among you? Don't they come from your desires that battle within you?" (James 4:1 NIV). To evaluate the problem biblically, we'll need to get to the heart. This is not something that will happen in just one meeting with Kylee. Our hearts' desires are often disguised or hidden. So plan to work patiently to help Kylee learn to see her heart. As you work over several weeks to learn what is happening internally, you may progress from answers such as, "I get mad when my brother takes my stuff because he ruins my things," to answers like this: "I don't like it when my brother ruins my things. If he ruins my clothes and shoes, we won't be able to afford to buy new things and the other girls at school won't think I'm cool. I'll have to wear clothes like Abby Dubronis wears, and I'll get made fun of."

Learning this affects our biblical evaluation of the problem. Kylee is not just a little girl who needs anger management instruction. Kylee is a little girl who fears being an outcast, who desires the approval of others, and who is motivated to do what it takes to make sure she doesn't suffer because others make fun of her.

Share Biblical Hope

In all of our counseling sessions we want to share biblical hope. In Kylee's world, the prospect of being made fun of is shattering. The only way she knows to guarantee not being abandoned and mocked by the other girls at school is to be cool.

Her source of hope is in being accepted by her classmates, and the threat of losing this has caused her to be angry and aggressive toward her little brother. Kylee doesn't have a hope that is big enough to get her through the third grade. Yet God offers her eternal hope, a hope so robust that it will not dry up and disappear when our suffering increases. As we share biblical hope, we have the privilege of leading Kylee to the Father of all compassion who sent his Son to rescue us from despair and give us a living hope that will never disappoint.

Kylee's fears of potential rejection are significant, as they would be for all of us. The raw pain of suffering can easily blind us to any comfort or encouragement. The first thing Kaylee may need to learn is to tell God what is happening and how hard it is. As she does this, she will take a first step in clinging to the One who, unlike her "friends," will never abandon her, will carry her sorrow, and will never show disdain for her.

As we continue to share biblical hope with Kylee, we'll also want to help her learn how powerful God is. You could possibly give Kylee homework to dramatize with her parents some of the Old Testament narratives that display God's power or some of the New Testament miracles where Jesus brings people back from the dead. The God who can do all these things can also protect Kylee's heart from the fear of what others think of her.

Kylee has a bigger purpose in life than escaping the disdain of her classmates. Kylee has been created to show how magnificent and beautiful God is—and that's even better than having other eight-year-olds think you're cool.

The curse of sin has brought suffering into Kylee's life. Other little girls make fun of those who don't live up to their standards. They are haughty toward classmates who can't afford to buy clothes like they wear. They persecute outsiders, and their tongues leave wounds that will be carried into adulthood.

But God invites Kylee, her parents, and all of us into a deeply intimate relationship with him. He won't ever judge us based on our shoes, our clothes, or any other aspect of our outward appearance. When our hearts are broken, he will be close. When our "friends" deeply wound us, he'll carry our sorrows.

God also offers to forgive those broken and oppressed by sin—those who feel uncontrollable anger wash over them and then carry the heavy burden of guilt as they look at the shards of a broken glass hurled in fear and anger. In those moments of guilt and shame, God offers the joy of forgiveness and the crown of compassion. We have a God who satisfies our desires with good things. We have hope!

Provide Biblical Instruction

As we learn the struggles and suffering experienced by the children we counsel, this should stir up compassion in us. One of the ways we demonstrate our compassion is to provide biblical instruction and help children to see Jesus. In Mark 6:34 we see Jesus himself responding to the helplessness and spiritual hunger of the crowds around him by taking time to teach them. We're told, "When Jesus landed and saw a large crowd, he had *compassion* on them, because they were like sheep without a shepherd. *So he began teaching them many things*" (NIV, emphasis mine).

This ties in directly to our goal for counseling. We want to use God's Word to lovingly help children we counsel become individuals who find God to be exceedingly magnificent, trustworthy, and good, and, as a result, live with the desire to be a more and more accurate image of his beauty by loving him and others. Although God's beauty may seem obvious to you, it may not be obvious to the child you counsel. The child may have all kinds of misperceptions about God.

As you gather relevant data, you'll want to learn the child's understanding of God. Maybe the child doesn't know God is good. Perhaps he or she has formed a picture of God as angry and eager to punish any disobedience. Perhaps the child has been threatened with God's wrath in order to keep him or her in line.

If this is the child's perception, promising that God will never leave or abandon those who belong to him won't provide hope or be attractive to the child. Who wants to always be with a deity looking for opportunities to punish you?

Perhaps the child doesn't think God is trustworthy. Perhaps someone quoted Psalm 91:9–16 to him when he was afraid, promising that God would never let any harm befall him if he trusted in the Lord. Later, when his grandmother died of cancer, the child decided God couldn't be trusted.[3] He doesn't understand that the "harm" God will not allow those who belong to him to suffer is something that would permanently damage their soul or separate them from him. All he knows is that his grandmother died, and God let it happen. God and his Word don't seem trustworthy.

Perhaps the child doesn't think God is all that magnificent. In the child's world, perhaps God's name is just a swear word for use when you're angry.

Gather data to learn the child's concept of God, and then use the richness of Old Testament narratives, the emotions of the psalms, and the Gospels' example of question and answer to provide biblical instruction about who God is. You may find that Kylee knows almost nothing about God. That means you get to introduce her to the living God!

Kylee's world has become a painful place. She has genuine struggles and is blundering in her attempts to control the circumstances in which she finds herself. Kylee needs to see the God who is powerful, trustworthy, and good.

Show the big picture

All of us were designed with the mission to show how beautiful and good and wonderful God is (e.g., Genesis 1:26–27; Isaiah 43:7; Romans 8:29; Ephesians 1:4, 11–13). Children need to know God made them to live for something much bigger than their best life now. They need to know God's purpose for their lives is to glorify him.

However, simply knowing our mission in life is not helpful if we don't also know how to fulfill it. According to Jesus, we fulfill our mission by loving God and loving others (Matthew 22:36–40).

Kylee has made it her mission to get the approval of others. But this hasn't led her to the peace she seeks. Her desires and choices have put her on a path of relational destruction with her brother, her parents, and even her classmates.

Contrast that with the way found in God's Word—it revives the soul, it makes simple people wise, it gives joy to the heart, it brings great reward (Psalm 19:7–11). As Kylee allows God and his Word to be her teacher, her dead soul can be brought back to life. Rather than throwing glasses to solve problems, she can grow in patience and learn to use her parents' help to address the problems with her brother. Rather than living with anxiety about being ostracized, her heart can trust God to care for her. And rather than fearing what she might lose if her classmates treat her with disdain, she can gain treasure more precious than gold (Psalm 19).

Assign Practical Homework

As we provide biblical instruction, we want to help the children we counsel practice these principles so they can be doers of the Word, not just hearers (James 1:22). Giving assignments at the end of the session for the children to practice during the week encourages them to see how these principles bear out in their real-life concerns.

As children learn to trust in Christ and put biblical teaching into practice, they will be equipped to stand against the storms of life coming against them (Matthew 7:24–27). While they may be battered by the storms of rejection, sexual temptation, abuse, or other forms of suffering and temptation, they won't be destroyed. Rather, they can join countless others in the confidence that God will one day bring an end to all that is wrong and that every tear will be wiped away from every eye.

As a general rule, I like to give children a "think" and "do" portion of each assignment to help solidify the concept we are working on. I use "think" assignments to review and expand what they are learning in the session and to help children evaluate which desires are influencing them. I use "do" assignments to help the children put the instruction into practice or to gather data.

As I begin to counsel Kylee, my first goal is to introduce Kylee to God, who made her and loves her. If I want to help Kylee see the goodness of God, her homework might look like this:

1. Read Psalm 119:68 out loud five times every day to someone in your family.
2. Bring two of your favorite gifts from God to show me in counseling next week. This could be a toy (like a doll or stuffed animal), it could be a food you like, it could be a picture of a friend, or it could be a favorite game you like to play.
3. Every day write down something to thank God for.
4. Write down any disappointments you had.

Here are some other starter ideas for assignments. Again, these are just to prime the pump. Some assignments are designed to help gather relevant data, some to help the child come closer to God, and some to help the child build relationships.

Assignments to gather relevant data might include:

- Draw a picture of the best thing in your life and the hardest thing in your life.
- Write or record a story about your day.
- Bring a playlist of the music you listened to most this week.
- Write a letter to the person who has been bullying you, saying what you are too scared to say to the bully. Bring it to counseling next time so we can talk about it.
- Keep a journal of upsets. Record what made you upset, what you did, and what you wanted.

Assignments to help the child come closer to God might include:

- Make up a cheer about how great God is.
- Review a relevant verse about God's character ten times every day.
- Act out the Old Testament story we discussed in counseling today and video it as you act it out.
- Listen to an assigned song (that teaches biblical truth) three times every day.
- Start a list of things you can thank God for. Add to this list every day.
- Cry out to God and ask him to help you.

Assignments to help the child build relationships and build better communication skills might include:

- Be ready to play your two favorite songs for me next time.
- Go on a walk with your parents and tell them what we discussed in counseling.
- Tell Mom and Dad the best part of your day when you come home from school each day.
- Ask your parents to pray with you. (This assignment is to encourage not only a relationship with God and the child's parents, but also to develop habits of having God as a natural part of the parent-child relationship.)
- Make a list of ten things you could do to be nice to your sibling. Do one of them each day.
- List ten things you can say when someone is mean to you at school.
- Introduce yourself to one person at school or church. Find out how many siblings they have.

Involve the Parents

My strong preference when counseling children is to make the parents part of the counseling session. There are several reasons for this.

1. The parents are the ones who will give an account to God for raising and training their children. While a counselor (teacher, coach, Sunday school teacher, or youth pastor) may provide great assistance with this, the parents are the ones commissioned with the nurture and instruction of their children. Therefore, they should be as much a part of the counseling process as possible.

2. Parents provide great insight into the child. They can explain what they observe in the life of the child. This can help you move in the right direction.

3. You want the parents to follow through with the child. As you teach principles in God's Word, you want the parents to know what has been taught so they can review, remind, and reinforce your teaching throughout the week.

4. You want to do everything you can to foster strong relationships between the parents and child. When parents aren't present during the counseling session, it tends to exclude them from relationship.

5. If the parents have been unsure how to help their child, you want to let them observe the things you teach and the ways you communicate. This helps equip them to be more effective parents.

6. You may gain opportunities to help the parents with some of their own struggles as they observe you helping their child.

If parents aren't part of the whole session, consider asking them to be present for the last ten minutes. Prepare the children for this and ask them if they would like to tell their parents what you have discussed so far. Ask the parents if they have any questions. It is important for the children to be present for this conversation so they hear everything you and their parents say. It also helps the parents set the example of how to productively communicate during conflict.

Of course, there may be times when the parents will need counsel themselves that is not about the children. In such situations, it would be appropriate to explain to the children that the reason for the meeting is for the parents to get help about a problem they have; the meeting is not to discuss the child behind his back.

The ideal outcome at the conclusion of counseling is that the child and the parents have taken steps toward finding God to be exceedingly magnificent, trustworthy, and good, and, as a result, they are living with the desire to be a more accurate image of his beauty by loving him and others, using the Word of God as their teacher.

CHAPTER 3

COUNSELING CHILDREN OF DIFFERENT AGE GROUPS: AGES AND STAGES OF DEVELOPMENT[1]

JULIE LOWE

Models of development guide professional interactions with children, whether it is among medical practitioners, education and learning specialists, or counselors. While several models are used, the following sample lists have been created for the purpose of one-on-one counseling ministry with children.

There are five developmental stages: early, middle, late childhood, young teen, and teenager. Such divisions are flexible and based on observing large populations of children. For this reason, we have broken out early childhood into two separate lists. Each stage has general milestones that give a sense for where a child might fall, but there is always a spectrum that allows for various rates of development. It is an ongoing process, to be regularly evaluated.

As always, it is essential to become an expert at knowing the child in front of you. You must wisely evaluate the child's development and if (or how) it might be influencing them. You are discerning where they are growing, but at a slower rate, or where they might be excelling, but still within a normal range. You are evaluating where they surpass their age range in certain areas of development, or where they may be significantly behind in ways that are detrimental and require intervention.

With time—and as we observe lifestyles, cultural norms, and patterns—we will also see changes in how children develop. For example, some research shows that children who spend more time on electronic devices often are slower in developing necessary hand strength. As a result, their ability to hold pencils, cut with scissors, string beads, color, or work puzzles is significantly delayed. Variables such as this are not always reflected in developmental guidelines, but they do impact how children are functioning.

Critical Implications for Counseling

All this is important for those who minister to or counsel children because developmental accelerations or delays often have emotional, social, and spiritual effects for young people. It impacts how they view themselves, compare themselves to others, or make sense out of their experiences. We must be prepared to help them navigate such things accurately.

For example, if a child is very concrete in his thinking, we will confuse him when we use metaphors and analogies he cannot comprehend. We tend to see this in young children, in kids on the autism spectrum, and even in teenagers who are literal and concrete by nature. We can frustrate them, and ourselves, by attempting to make them think abstractly.

Likewise, if a child has a short attention span but we force her to sit, talk, and focus for longer than is loving, we create frustration, an unpleasant atmosphere, and a resistance in her to return or engage with us.

There are children who feel intimidated by direct eye contact and who would open up much more quickly if we provided a distraction (such as an activity, or simply drawing or building something) while talking. They engage with less effort and more vulnerability when given something to do with their hands. Activities that draw young people out can be very useful and fruitful.[2]

Our knowledge of children must also inform how we approach them and engage in conversation. Ministering to and speaking into the lives of young people requires us to do our best to make our words as winsome, clear, and attractive to them as possible. I often see children and teens who are weak in processing information. If we do not adapt our interactions, we lose them in conversation. They miss what we are saying. When children do not understand, they will often just nod or let us continue talking. Sometimes (but not often) a young person will actually tell us when they don't understand; for the most part, many simply placate us. They don't want to look foolish, so they don't ask. Instead, they tune us out—and we may write them off as unwilling or rebellious, when in reality they simply don't comprehend what we're telling them. We want to take the responsibility to find open doors into their world and to both draw them out and speak back in effectively.

I do not believe development directs everything we do; it simply helps build a bigger, better picture of the child as a whole. Development, temperament, and innate traits and characteristics do not determine a person's life. It is imperative that our observations are informed by a biblical worldview— one that views young people as image-bearers; understands human nature; and acknowledges our inherent bent toward sin and how our bodies and development are impacted by sin and weakness, suffering and brokenness.

As children and teens develop, they are forming views of identity, self-understanding, normalcy and values, relationships (with man and God), and moral decision-making. We also know that we all process life and our experiences differently, and often inaccurately. Children need wisdom outside themselves; they need help understanding who they are before the Lord and how to live in a broken world. When they look or feel different than peers, when they cannot keep up with those around them, or when they are not accepted for their differences, we need to point them to a Creator who helps make sense of their experiences.

Learning to understand both development and the nature of the human heart will help you develop wisdom in putting the pieces of the puzzle together and helping young people.

Early Childhood Milestones (ages 3–4)

Physical

- ✓ Learns to hold utensils and writing tools
- ✓ Draws lines and circles
- ✓ Runs, skips, climbs independently
- ✓ Can pedal
- ✓ Able to start dressing themselves
- ✓ Demonstrates dominant hand
- ✓ Can use toilet on their own
- ✓ Is aware of gender

Emotional

- ✓ Can tell what is real and make-believe
- ✓ Shows more independence and preferences
- ✓ Perceives world from self point of view
- ✓ Likes to imitate parents or caregivers
- ✓ Identifies basic emotions
- ✓ Identity and security established by caregivers
- ✓ Becoming more social and likes making friends

Cognitive

- ✓ Can count to ten or more
- ✓ More literal and concrete in understanding
- ✓ Talks in sentences
- ✓ Unable to see perspectives other than own
- ✓ Begins to understand cause and effect
- ✓ Can formulate own ideas and questions
- ✓ Recites songs, rhymes, and simple stories
- ✓ Shows own preferences, likes, and dislikes
- ✓ Can complete puzzles and memory games
- ✓ Attention span often 5–10 minutes

Social

- ✓ Inner world is expressed through play
- ✓ Enters into role-play
- ✓ Can follow simple games and simple rules
- ✓ Learns to take turns
- ✓ Begins to learn cooperation and sharing
- ✓ Bonds with a friend
- ✓ Notices the physical world around them
- ✓ Tests authority, demonstrates own will

Spiritual

- ✓ Learns right and wrong by example
- ✓ Conscience is undeveloped, shaped by what is modeled
- ✓ Obedience toward God is patterned in obedience to parents
- ✓ Understands simple truths in concrete ways
- ✓ Literal understanding of God, heaven, sin, obedience, kindness, and sharing
- ✓ Good and bad behavior often understood through attached consequences

Helpful Resources:

- ✓ Puppet sand miniatures
- ✓ Role-play scenarios and tools
- ✓ Art materials: blank paper, markers, crayons, glue, etc.
- ✓ Dollhouse for identifying family roles, rules, patterns
- ✓ Musical instruments for self-expression
- ✓ Books, pictures, and the use of storytelling to deliver messages and understanding

Early Childhood Milestones (ages 5–6)

Physical

- ✓ Speaks clearly
- ✓ Shares simple stories
- ✓ Greater use of imagination

- ✓ Able to learn to ride a bike

- ✓ Can fully dress themselves
- ✓ Able to tie shoes
- ✓ Begins to learn letters and shapes

Emotional

- ✓ Can begin to demonstrate empathy
- ✓ Shows more independence and preferences

- ✓ Shows wide range of emotions

- ✓ Becoming more social and likes making friends

- ✓ Learning impulse control
- ✓ Anxiety and emotions demonstrate in play and fantasy

- ✓ Reality and fantasy can blend together
- ✓ Starts to verbalize feelings of doubt, guilt, shame, embarrassment

Cognitive

- ✓ Greater awareness of outside world
- ✓ Greater awareness of cause and effect outside of themselves
- ✓ Can tell what is real and make-believe

- ✓ Can begin to do simple problem solving

- ✓ Follows multiple steps/ directions
- ✓ Growing sense of time

- ✓ Remember words and events associated with touching, smelling, and hearing, as well as with emotions (both pleasant and fearful)
- ✓ Attention span averages 10–15 minutes

Social

- ✓ Learning cooperation in groups

- ✓ May be part of a group but not interact much because they see themselves first

- ✓ Enjoys structured play and games

- ✓ Can follow rules and likes to make others follow them

- ✓ Wants everything to be fair—this is where temper tantrums may come in

- ✓ Shows more independence in relationship-building

- ✓ Relationships built on common likes

- ✓ Wants to be liked and accepted

- ✓ Can begin to exhibit competition

Spiritual

- ✓ Knows that the Bible is an important book about God's people and Jesus

- ✓ Enjoys stories about Jesus and likes to hear stories over and over again

- ✓ Asks many questions: Where is God? Does he eat? Who made God? Why is God invisible?

- ✓ Learns easy, simple prayers

- ✓ Can be encouraged to give their own offering to God and the church

- ✓ Develops a sense of church community and attendance

- ✓ Benefits from accepting adults who are willing to hear their many questions

- ✓ Relies on authority for their moral compass

- ✓ Conscience regarding sin and behavior is developing

- ✓ Experiencing and enjoying God's world

Helpful Resources:

- ✓ Art Materials: colored pencils, crayons, markers, glue, simple crafts

- ✓ Books and stories that help delve into and reaffirm a message/truth

✓ Object lessons to help deliver a message or truth

✓ Puppets, miniatures, or dollhouses/sand trays—role-playing and personal application

✓ Simple games for asking questions, role-playing, or real-life scenarios to work through

✓ Musical instruments for telling or creating their own stories or songs

✓ Other concrete ways to convey the message/truth you want to affirm

Middle Childhood Milestones (ages 7–9)

Physical

- ✓ Have adult teeth and growing appetite
- ✓ Active and enjoys sports/ activities
- ✓ Improved coordination and strength

- ✓ Able to draw more complex pictures with objects, people, and animals

- ✓ Handwriting and hand-eye coordination improves
- ✓ Speech is clear and vocabulary increases greatly
- ✓ With growing numbers of kids, puberty may develop (around age 9)

Emotional

- ✓ Likes affection and affirmation from adults

- ✓ Peer influence is growing and shaping likes/dislikes

- ✓ Can articulate many emotions and feelings

- ✓ Growing autonomy from parents in many skills and abilities
- ✓ Demonstrates greater ability to control impulses and think before acting
- ✓ May be more argumentative and willful

Cognitive

- ✓ Can begin to understand more abstract ideas
- ✓ Can think more systematically; able to generalize what is learned
- ✓ Considers more questions and becomes more curious about life
- ✓ Amply verbal

- ✓ Enjoys humor and laughter

- ✓ Increases ability to recall events and remember sequence

- ✓ Able to spell out words and read books
- ✓ Attention span varies but averages 15 minutes

Social

- ✓ Often will prefer same-sex peer group
- ✓ Enjoys social interactions and group activities
- ✓ Leadership and status in social groups begin to emerge
- ✓ Begins to look for sense of belonging in the peer group

- ✓ Wants peer approval
- ✓ Can enjoy time alone
- ✓ Group identity affirmed by likes: sports, music, art
- ✓ Begins to form hobbies and interests

Spiritual

- ✓ Will be curious, asking never-ending questions while exploring God's world
- ✓ Practices love and trust as a result of parents or other significant adults; begins to understand God's love
- ✓ Learns that parents obey God, and that they too must obey God
- ✓ Develops empathy and love for others and toward new people
- ✓ Imitates and repeats what a parent does
- ✓ Consistency becomes one of the most important qualities for moral and spiritual development

- ✓ Able to see battle to see things "my way" or "God's way"
- ✓ Can be rule-oriented (i.e., "follow the rules and you are good"—instead of "Jesus makes us good")
- ✓ Strong sense of fairness; proneness to being pharisaical
- ✓ Personal relationship to God develops, exhibited by asking God for help, change, do what's right
- ✓ Recognizes others' poor behavior and sin

Helpful Resources:

✓ Working with concrete objects, instead of just images

✓ Stories and books that capture the interest of the child and help develop a sense of wonder and awe

✓ Art materials, to continue to draw out and engage with ideas

✓ Creating spaces or worlds (fantasy or real) to engage with hard feelings, events, or ideas

✓ Storytelling through song, music, books, role-play

✓ Concrete projects/ideas/ homework for parents, to practice new truths or things they are learning in the home or school environment

✓ Creative tools like balls or Jenga that have questions and role-playing scenarios—fosters conversation and processing of hard things while doing something enjoyable

Late Childhood Milestones (ages 10–12)

Physical

- ✓ Energetic and active

- ✓ Height and weight increase progressively
- ✓ Body begins to go through changes
- ✓ Developing body proportions similar to those of an adult

- ✓ May begin puberty—evident sexual development, voice changes, and increased body odor are common
- ✓ Skin becomes oiler and may develop pimples
- ✓ Hair grows in various areas of the body

Emotional

- ✓ Fluctuates between confidence and insecurity
- ✓ Begins to define self by the way others see them
- ✓ Ability to see differing views

- ✓ Greater fluctuating emotions and moodiness
- ✓ Distinguishes between will, actions, and motives
- ✓ Is more aware of strengths and weaknesses

Cognitive

- ✓ Increased ability to learn and apply skills

- ✓ Establishes abstract thinking skills, but reverts to concrete thought under stress
- ✓ Not yet able to make all intellectual leaps, like inferring a hypothetical motive or reason

- ✓ View of the world extends beyond a black-white/right-wrong perspective
- ✓ Interpretative ability develops

- ✓ Able to answer who, what, where, and when questions, but still may have problems with why questions

✓ Learns to extend thinking beyond personal experiences and knowledge

✓ Attention span varies widely; averages 20 minutes at a time

Social

✓ Increased ability to interact with peers

✓ Often struggles with relating to peers, either by being controlled or trying to control peers

✓ Looks for acceptance through peer group

✓ Increased capacity to engage in competition

✓ Has a strong group identity; increasingly defines self through peers

✓ Sense of accomplishment based upon the achievement of increased strength and self-control

✓ Shows more interest in the opposite sex

✓ Imagines self as an adult and independent

✓ Defines self-concept in part by success in school

✓ Able to understand and engage with the emotions and struggles of others

✓ Able to learn and apply conflict resolution skills

Spiritual

✓ Develops and tests values and beliefs that will guide present and future behaviors

✓ Aware of internal conscience and motives influencing choices and behaviors

✓ Pursuit of God's help often linked to meeting needs and help with relationships

✓ Struggles how to think and respond to being sinned against by others

✓ Begins questioning rules, while maintaining that rules are important and to be followed

✓ Struggles to know how God sees them versus how others see them

Spiritual

- ✓ Identifies discrepancies in values of others and compares/contrasts them to own values
- ✓ Can discern between their desires toward sin and desire to follow God
- ✓ Needs to be taught how to pray and what to expect when they pray

Helpful Resources:

- ✓ Journaling and self-reflection activities
- ✓ Question-asking games
- ✓ Games that foster godly conflict resolution and working through difficult situations
- ✓ Role-playing exercises
- ✓ Bible studies and resources that foster personal relationship with the Lord
- ✓ Worksheets and group activities that facilitate mature discussions of hard issues
- ✓ Storytelling; testimonies; real, personal examples of change, faith, and growth
- ✓ Strategic games that work on problem solving
- ✓ Art materials and resources

Young Teen Milestones (ages 13–14)

Physical

- ✓ Hormones change as puberty begins
- ✓ More concerned about physical changes and appearance
- ✓ Eating increases and changes, and at times eating problems develop
- ✓ Physical activity important for health and general mood
- ✓ Requires more sleep, but often resists it
- ✓ Development of sexual organs and voice change

Emotional

- ✓ Experiences more moodiness
- ✓ Demonstrates more concern about appearance, body image, looks
- ✓ Feels more stress and pressure to perform in school
- ✓ Sadness, depression, anxiety related to school performance, peer acceptance, or parental expectations
- ✓ Able to express feelings and talk through them

Cognitive

- ✓ Have more ability for complex thought
- ✓ Able to be abstract
- ✓ Holds own opinions and begins to turn to peers to inform them
- ✓ Needs help considering long-term consequences for choices/decisions, rather than short-term benefits

Social

- ✓ Significantly driven by the value of their peer group
- ✓ Proactive relationship-building with adults is not valued, but much needed

✓ Friendships formed around feelings of who accepts them and where they fit in

✓ Desires autonomy from parents and greater dependence on peer group

✓ Forms connections and bonds over social media

Spiritual

✓ Begins to realize choices are complex and that they can choose to sin

✓ Rules may or may not be important—temptation to feel they can judge morality

✓ May understand the letter of the law more than the spirit of the law

✓ Personal relationship with the Lord must lead to decisions/ choices

✓ Develops stronger individual values and morals

✓ Will question more ideas

✓ May express discomfort praying out loud, and need help learning to pray and knowing what to expect when they pray

✓ Learning to take responsibility for own actions, decisions, and consequences

Helpful Resources:

✓ Question-asking exercises and activities

✓ Resources that help develop good decision-making and godly values

✓ Art activities and resources for self-expression and self-awareness

✓ Activity or exercises that encourage self-expression of feelings, thoughts, and values

✓ Genuine interest in hearing their opinions, likes, dislikes

✓ Forming trust/mutual respect by engaging with or entering their world—social media, art, athletics, hobbies, other interests

Teenage Milestones (ages 15–18)

Physical

✓ Physical abilities at their peak

✓ Completion of puberty from childhood

✓ Females tend to reach adult height, while males continue to grow

✓ Increased muscle strength, reaction time, cardio functioning, and sensory abilities

✓ Changes of skin, vision, and reproductive ability

✓ Begins expressing sexuality in various ways

✓ Requires more sleep and proper nutrition

✓ Greater physical independence: learns to drive, gets a job, spends time with friends

Emotional

✓ Can articulate their own feeling and analyze why they feel a certain way

✓ Wrestles with understanding what drives their emotions/ motives

✓ Develops their own personality and opinions

✓ Attributes values on appearance, talents, and personality

✓ Capable of intense emotions and mood changes

Cognitive

✓ Decision-making is still developing

✓ Learning choices have risks and consequences

✓ Builds self-sufficiency skills

✓ Sometimes struggles to think through risks and consequences of actions

✓ Brain still developing and maturing

✓ Forms well-defined work habits

✓ Considers and makes plans for the future: school, college, job

Social

- ✓ Demonstrates loyalty to peer group

- ✓ Desires increased independence from parents/family

- ✓ Influenced by choices, values, and habits of peer group

- ✓ More concerns about body image and clothes

- ✓ Greater capacity for caring for others

- ✓ Challenges parental authority, with desire to be more autonomous

- ✓ Has the capacity to form deep, mutual, healthy relationships

- ✓ Influenced by cultural values and messages

- ✓ Greater ability to sense right and wrong

- ✓ May feel more sadness and emotion—can lead to poor grades, use of addictive substances, and other problems

Spiritual

- ✓ Wants ways to make faith relevant to life

- ✓ Confused by cultural norms and values versus biblical values

- ✓ Corporate worship and church attendance critical to shaping values and forming a personal relationship with Christ

- ✓ May express discomfort praying out loud, and needs help learning to pray and knowing what to expect when they pray

- ✓ Godly, healthy adult relationships vital to spiritual development

- ✓ Needs modeling of how to deal with peer pressure and issues of addiction, sexuality, and suicide

- ✓ Benefits from adult-led discussions and opportunities to ask questions

Helpful Resources:

- ✓ Question-asking exercises and activities

- ✓ Resources that help develop good decision-making and mature choices

- ✓ Resources that instill godly values and mature relationships

- ✓ Stories, testimonies, and personal examples of people who have overcome hard issues teens face, providing examples that guide toward godliness and faith

- ✓ Art activities and resources for self-expression and self-awareness

- ✓ Activity or exercises that encourage self-expression of feelings, thoughts, and values

- ✓ Genuine interest in hearing their opinions, likes, dislikes

- ✓ Forming trust/mutual respect by engaging with or entering their world—social media, art, athletics, hobbies, other interests

- ✓ Creating places of supportive community

- ✓ Fostering safe discussion and opportunity for questions on topics of peer friendships, drugs and alcohol, sex, depression, and suicide

Part 2

Specific Counseling Issues

Children and Their Relationships

CHAPTER 4
LEADING CHILDREN TO JESUS[1]
MARTY MACHOWSKI

A ten-year-old girl, Samantha, sat nervously in my office. She twisted her hair around her fingers as she explained that she didn't think she was a Christian even though she had "accepted" Jesus many times. Her mom came with her for counseling because every time Samantha heard an altar call, she went forward, but she didn't seem to understand the gospel or what it means to follow Jesus. Samantha was close with her mom and didn't seem to mind her sitting in.

After talking with Samantha over several sessions, I found out more about her, her family, and what her ideas are about what it means to be a Christian. She is the youngest of four children. Her two older sisters and older brother are confident they are Christians, and in her eyes they seem to have it all together. Her father is a pastor, and her mom a homemaker. They have daily devotions and pray together. Lately her parents have been asking Samantha to have her own devotions. So she does read the Bible, but she can't make sense of it and has no idea what to read or why to read it. She also has some secret sins that she finally confesses: She often doesn't do her homework and lies to her parents and her teachers about it. She also has stolen a few things from her friends and her sisters (clothes, of course!). She is ashamed and doubts whether a "real" Christian would do such things.

Where to Start?

While ultimately it is the work of the Holy Spirit to soften a child's heart and lead him or her to repentance and faith, the Lord gives us the privilege of joining in the work he is doing. Bringing children to Christ is a walk of trust, a journey to pass along the life-giving message of the cross and resurrection.

The most important and foundational relationship in a child's life is his or her relationship with the Lord. Although children will have varying levels of ability to comprehend the Lord and their dependence on him—dependent on their ages and stages of development—we know the key orientation of their lives is going to stem from how they understand their need for a right relationship with their Creator. This understanding will shape how they view their purpose, how they form life goals, and where they find their core identity.

You don't need to be specially trained in order to share the gospel effectively with children. The Bible offers the same gospel to adults and children alike, and in fact urges us to come to God like little children (Matthew 18:2–4). God wants us to have an expectant faith that the gospel is powerful and that it can revolutionize the lives of the young people we love. The great preacher, Charles Spurgeon, said it well, "The things that are essential to salvation are so exceedingly simple that no child need sit down in despair of understanding the things which make for his peace. Christ crucified is not a riddle for sages, but a plain truth for plain people. True, it is meat for men, but it is also milk for babes."[2]

From the earliest ages, children can begin to understand that they have been made by a loving God for the purpose of glorifying and loving him forever (Genesis 1). As they grow in awareness, they need to see that their relationship with God has been broken and fragmented by sin, resulting in death (Genesis 3), and no amount of doing good or keeping rules will fix things (Romans 3:10–20). Hand in hand with these grave realities, children then need to hear the very best news of all, that Jesus paid the full penalty for their sin by his death on the cross, opening the way for them to become children of God (Romans 3:22–26). The call to them is the same call to all of us: confess and believe (Romans 10:9).

These are all important truths to share with any child to help them understand the gospel and their need for Jesus. But different children will have different struggles with faith and will need to hear different aspects of the gospel emphasized. In Samantha's case, there seemed to be a basic (and common) misunderstanding—she believed she had to become a good person before she could become a Christian.

Calling Samantha to faith had to start by sharing that the gospel is for sinners and reminding her that everyone has sinned and fallen short of the glory of God (Romans 3:23). Even Samantha's parents and siblings were sinners. I shared with her that Jesus said he came for sinners, not for good people (Matthew 9:13). The most important thing for entrance into God's kingdom is to know that we are sinners who need saving.

Belief and Repentance

But Samantha, like all children and adults, needed to be called to repentance *and* faith in Jesus. We shouldn't call children to faith without also calling them to repentance (turning away from sin). Repentance from our sin and faith in Christ are a part of the same gospel call. Repentance means you were going away from God, but then, by God's grace, you turned away from your sin, toward God. It is true that we each grow in our level of repentance as we are gradually made more like Jesus, but there is a turning from our sin that takes place in our initial response to the gospel. Wayne Grudem explains it like this: "Any genuine gospel proclamation must include an invitation to make a conscious decision to forsake one's sins and come to Christ in faith, asking Christ for forgiveness of sins. If either the need to repent of sins or the need to trust in Christ for forgiveness is neglected, there is not a full and true proclamation of the gospel."[3]

It is not until a child comes to Christ as Savior and places their full trust in the work of Christ that they are saved. This trust is a personal decision of their heart, the very core of their being. We want to be careful that understanding, approving, and trusting in Christ are all present in a child's life and profession.

> When we realize that genuine saving faith must be accompanied by genuine repentance for sin, it helps us to understand why some preaching of the gospel has such inadequate results today. If there is no mention of the need for repentance, sometimes the gospel message becomes only, "Believe in Jesus Christ and be saved" without any mention of repentance at all. But this watered-down version of the gospel does not ask for a wholehearted commitment to Christ—commitment *to* Christ, if genuine, must include a commitment to turn *from* sin. Preaching the need for faith without repentance is preaching only half of the gospel.[4]

It was important for Samantha to know that repentance for sins was an ongoing need in her life, since sin is also ongoing in all of us until we meet Jesus face-to-face. Although it was important for her to confess to Jesus her sins of lying and stealing, it was also important for her to know that being a Christian does not mean we are free of sin. Instead, it means we have an ongoing need to go to Jesus for daily help and forgiveness (Romans 7:21–25). God strengthens us to grow in obeying like Jesus did, and this helps us grow in the likeness of our Savior and King.

To help Samantha understand exactly what "going her own way" looked and sounded like in her life, we talked together about Jesus saying that what we do and say comes out of what is in our hearts (Matthew 15:18–19). We discussed together what might have been in her heart that resulted in her stealing and lying. Because she had a hard time understanding that people who looked good on the outside were sinners as well, I made sure to share my own sins and struggles with her.

It is also important to teach children what it means to believe. The apostle Paul uses the expression "believe in your heart" to describe how we are to trust in the saving work of Christ (Romans 10:9–10). Believing is more than merely consenting to the truth of the facts of the gospel, however. Believing is not only knowing; it is completely trusting in Jesus. We should be careful not to trivialize belief with statements like, "All you have to do is accept Jesus into your heart." Better to use biblical appeals based on Scriptures like those in Acts. "Repent therefore, and turn back, that your sins may be blotted out" (Acts 3:19); or "I preached that they should repent and turn to God and demonstrate their repentance by their deeds" (Acts 26:20 NIV). Notice that these biblical appeals require both faith and repentance.

Samantha and I talked about how having faith means putting all of our trust in Jesus. To illustrate, I took a chair and sat down without putting my full weight on the chair; instead, I hovered above the seat. I asked her if I really trusted that the chair would hold me up. She agreed that I didn't. Then we talked about what putting her full "weight" on Jesus might look and sound like in her life.

We also talked together about the hope we have in Jesus. Children, just like adults, are troubled about their sins and wonder what will happen to them when they die. I wanted Samantha to know that the gospel is a hope-filled message that gives sinners like us the only way to be forgiven and free, and live forever with God.

The Fruit of Faith

As you counsel children and talk with them about faith, it's important to remember that God is often at work drawing children to himself multiple times prior to their conversion. Their journey of faith may not be one linear path with an immediate, clear-cut trajectory to salvation. Parents and others who minister to children sometimes too quickly celebrate an early affirmation of the gospel as a full conversion to Christ—before they see true change. Later this can cause confusion in the life of a teen who isn't living for God but thinks he is a Christian solely based on the fact that he raised his hand at the end of a meeting. That is what happened to Jay. The following is an excerpt from his story:

I grew up in a Christian home, went to church every Sunday, attempting to live the way I thought was right. At the age of seven, I prayed the sinner's prayer at a Vacation Bible School and pledged my life to Jesus. In the years that followed, I didn't really know what I was getting into, but I knew that it wasn't what I expected. I knew I wanted something, but I didn't know what it was or where to find it—but I knew it was out there.

It wasn't until seven years later, at my second year at youth camp, that I experienced God. The speaker talked about God's love in dying for our sins upon the cross, and how much we need it. I felt really moved by this and accepted Christ, this time for real. This included me confessing my sin and my need to walk in repentance. I made my commitment to Christ so that I could live my life for him, and so I could share my faith and tell other people about the gospel.

Jay's Vacation Bible School teachers thought he had become a Christian back when he was seven and excitedly reported back to his parents that Jay had raised his hand. Jay's parents were glad and affirmed his response, but opted to wait and see what God was doing in his life before they considered whether he was demonstrating a genuine understanding of the gospel and the fruit of new life. Jay thought he had pledged his life to Jesus as a seven-year-old, but it wasn't until he was a teenager that God opened his eyes to see his personal need for the gospel. He would say this is when he was truly converted and his life began to change.

As Jay's pastor, I got to watch God's work from a front-row seat. Prior to camp, Jay was a good kid, but he didn't show much affection for God. After his experience at camp, however, Jay's whole life changed. He turned from his sin and began pursuing God. He and another young man gathered their friends to study the Bible and various Christian books to learn more about God. It was easy to see the fruit of Jay's changed life.

While you can't thwart a true conversion by responding cautiously, you can give a child false assurance of where they stand with God. This is where parents, ministers, and counselors can make mistakes. Too often we ask children if they want to make Jesus their "forever friend" and then tell them they are a Christian if they answer yes. This is what happened in Samantha's case. She had "prayed the prayer," but her conscience was troubled by her ongoing sins. She needed to have a deeper understanding of what it meant to be a Christian and to live a life of ongoing faith and repentance. As she learned what it meant to follow Jesus, she grew in her confidence that she belonged to him. That gave her the freedom to confess her sins to her parents and others and to believe in the forgiveness of sins based on Jesus's sacrifice for her. Salvation isn't something she could do or earn, even by praying a prayer. Salvation is something God does. We repent, we trust in Jesus, we pray, but the Spirit of God does the saving.

Remember that kids love to respond to our teaching, but that doesn't mean the Spirit of God is yet touching their lives. There is a lot more to the gospel than Jesus becoming their friend. I've counseled many families with struggling teens who, because of a childhood response, believed they were Christians but now felt no need for the gospel. If they were honest, many teens in this situation would admit they had never lived for Christ, nor experienced affections for the

Lord, his Word, or the people of God. We have many kids who call themselves Christians but have not yet experienced lives transformed by the Spirit of God. Helping them see their sin and need for Christ is the first step in leading them to genuinely repent and turn their hearts toward Jesus.

That doesn't mean young children can't become genuine believers. My wife, Lois, first repented of her sins at age five in response to her mom sharing the gospel with her. After hearing the gospel message that day, the Spirit of God convicted her young heart. This is clear in hindsight, but her conversion couldn't be confirmed until her life demonstrated that she was turning away from her sin and living for Jesus. While we pray God will save our children at a young age, and they will proclaim the gospel from the time they can talk, we should be patient to wait for the changed life that results from genuine repentance, which always flows from a child transformed by the gospel.

A Word to Parents

Often parents stumble in the process of leading a child toward Christ because of fear: fear of failure, fear of a child's lack of response, or fear that it's up to them to say just the right words. These fears can lead you to try to save a child yourself, instead of trusting that the Spirit of God is in charge of exactly when a child will grow in faith. Fear can even lead parents to think a child is converted prematurely or, conversely, to give up when they don't see the changes they were hoping for.

On the other hand, complacency can steal the show when parents don't take seriously their calling to share the good news of the gospel with children, preferring to "let go and let God."

Instead of fear or complacency, you can be directed by your understanding of the gospel of Jesus Christ and the Spirit of Christ. Your own encounters with the good news of Jesus, your experience of repentance and grace, and the indwelling power of the Holy Spirit will be a powerful catalyst for sharing gospel hope with your child. If you can articulate to a listening child your need for Christ, this opens the door for your children to see their own need for placing their faith in Jesus as Savior.

As adults, the gospel message should continue to affect our hearts. After all, these are incredible truths! When you are freshly touched by the ongoing work of the Spirit of God in your personal Bible reading or during a message, share those moments with the children in your life.

It really helps our children to hear about how God is at work in our lives. Sharing how you had to confess to a friend that you gossiped, or lied, and how God is helping you change will show children repentance in action.

Also remember that you want to communicate the same compassion for a child's sins that God demonstrates toward them in their sin. God does not treat us as our sins deserve. He removes our sin as far away as the east is from the west (Psalm 103:10–12).

When we see confession of sin, profession of Christ, or a change in sinful patterns of behavior, we should encourage our children and alert them to the grace of God at work in their lives. At some point, their faith in Christ will become obvious as you regularly encourage them and direct them back to the gospel. Try not to miss these opportunities to help them acknowledge what God is doing in them.

Be encouraged that while you pray, read the Bible with your children, and wait for God to work, the Spirit is at work in ways you can't always see. This happened to my wife and also with our daughter. We had begun to see evidence of faith in the life of our daughter Emma, but it wasn't until we read the following testimony she wrote that we discovered exactly how it happened:

> As I grew older, I started to question whether or not I really was a Christian because I didn't find pleasure in reading the Bible or spending time with the Lord. Around age thirteen, the evening after hearing a message preached to the youth, I got up in the middle of the night, feeling the weight of my sin. I went into our bathroom and got down on my knees, and I told God that I wouldn't stop praying until he lifted the weight off of my shoulders. I told him that I believed that his Son had come and died for my sins and that if I trusted in him I would have eternal life. I cried and prayed for at least twenty minutes, begging the Lord to save me from my sins.
>
> After I was done praying, I got up, and I was sure that God had forgiven me, a sinner, and that Jesus had died on the cross for my sins, therefore giving me the gift of eternal life. I wanted to go outside and yell out to the whole world that the Lord had died for me and forgiven me of my transgressions. I can now say without a doubt that I am a Christian saved by the grace of God.

My wife and I had no knowledge of Emma's wrestling with God, so it was easy in reading her testimony to realize that we didn't convert our daughter—God did. Remembering that God is the one who saves a child keeps us from feeling pride and crediting our great counseling or good parenting for their salvation. In the same way, knowing only God can save spares us the condemnation that can affect us when our children continue in their rebellion and are slow to change.

When we understand that our job is to share the gospel, while God is the one who does the saving, we can do our part and then relax as parents and mentors while we watch God work. Let's regain the important truth that the gospel is "the power of God" (Romans 1:16) for our salvation. By sharing a clear gospel message each and every week, we can be faithful to the charge of Jesus, who said, "Let the little children come to me and do not hinder them, for to such belongs the kingdom of heaven" (Matthew 19:14).

CHAPTER 5
Navigating Parent/Child Relationships
Jessica Thompson

Maguire's relationship with his parents has never been easy. He remembers arguing with them about anything and everything since he was little. Now strife characterizes their every interaction with each other—it has become almost a daily habit to disagree about every plan, every goal, and every preference. Their normal mode of relating to each other is to each dig their heels into the ground and fight for their way. When they talk to each other, Maguire feels like his parents never hear a word he says so he vacillates between either not talking at all or yelling at them to try and get his point across. He is convinced they are too strict. No other parents he knows demand straight As. No other parents he knows limits to one hour per day the time their kids can spend on electronic devices. He often argues that he can't even get his homework research done in one hour. Maguire has recently started sneaking out to friends' houses so he can use their phone or computer to connect with other friends and to feel like he is a part of the group.

Maguire's parents, Janet and Tim, believe he is more defiant, stubborn, and strong-willed than any other teenager they know, and that these traits have characterized his personality from early on. He challenged them constantly as he grew up—about the time to eat, the time for bed, and which clothes he would wear for the day. Maguire's parents knew they had high expectations regarding his behavior, but they say that was because he was really smart. He was talking and reading before all the other children his age, and he could articulate his interest in a variety of topics. They knew he was completely capable of listening to their directions and understanding their guidelines, but that he just didn't care.

Janet and Tim both had incredibly hard childhoods and basically had to survive on their own. They can't understand why Maguire is always acting up when he has things so easy in comparison. However, because being second best would have never enabled them to climb out of poverty and make a better life for themselves, they hold both of their children to an incredibly high standard of behavior and performance. Sheila, their daughter, is the classic first child overachiever, both an honors student and a star player on her high school soccer and basketball teams. Janet and Tim know Maguire is also capable of rising to the challenge, if he only cared.

Maguire is now fifteen years old and a freshman in high school. He vacillates between feeling invisible to his parents and feeling like their biggest obsession. He knows that he isn't exactly giving what he could in terms of working for grades, taking personal responsibility, and caring about his general attitude toward his parents. He doesn't even always understand why he can't just be an easygoing kid. He knows that if he were just a little more compliant it would be better for everyone, but he never wants to back down when his parents push him. He just isn't interested in the things his parents want him to care about. He has said to his parents that he will never be as good as they want him to be, and that he will never be as good as Sheila.

Under the surface of this strife, Maguire is consumed with replaying his dad's words from a baseball game two years ago. He struck out for the final out of a playoff game. He can still see his dad's look of disappointment and then hear him say, "You never try at anything! Take life more seriously." At that time he looked over at his mom and saw her shaking her head.

The only place Maguire finds some peace is in the church youth group. His parents make him go every week, but he would actually go even if they didn't force him. The youth pastor is kind and encouraging, and Maguire doesn't feel like he has to do anything special to be accepted by peers there. He believes all of the truth the youth pastor teaches, but he isn't sure how these Christian principles can change his relationship with his parents. He feels like it is impossible to just obey, and he doesn't think anybody understands how he feels.

Part of the family guidelines at home are that Tim and Janet will look through their kids' backpacks and rooms at least twice a month. In one of the most recent sweeps, Tim found a condom in Maguire's backpack. It was still wrapped, but Tim was furious. One of the most prominent rules of their household was that premarital sex was off limits. When Tim confronted him about the condom, Maguire promised he wasn't having sex but that a friend had given it to him and he had felt dumb saying he didn't want it. Tim and Janet didn't believe him. Tim replied to Maguire, "Your mom and I are done with you. If you insist on ruining your life, then you go ahead. We are done trying to help you."

After this most recent outburst, Janet decided to reach out for some outside help. She can see that their relationship with Maguire is completely deteriorating, but she doesn't know what to do differently. She has convinced Tim to attend a counseling session, albeit begrudgingly. Maguire is also with them. He acts indifferent about being there, but inwardly he hopes the counselor will see the situation from his side and tell his parents to ease up on him.

The Struggle Is Not Against Flesh and Blood

Parents and children alike often feel they are in a bitter struggle against each other. Parents want respect and obedience. Children want freedom and independence. These two desires clash in most parent-child relationships, even in the households with the healthiest dynamics. In all families there is a level of tension and a pull to navigate the issues of authority versus emerging independence. What parents and children both need to understand as they sort out this issue is that neither the parent nor the child is the true enemy. Moms, dads, children, and teens all have a true and common enemy, what Ephesians 6:12 refers to as "the powers of this dark world and . . . the spiritual forces of evil" (NIV). This concept may sound otherworldly and not at all practical, but the reality is if we can get our counselees to think outside of their present situation and to put the parent-child relationship in its proper context, it will encourage a helpful perspective that will motivate pursuing a healthy bond. If you can help families look up long enough to take a breath and see their relationships are more complex than what they see, it may help them have a more objective view of the deeper issues at work.

Interestingly, this spiritual warfare passage from Ephesians is from the same chapter that delves deeply into family relationships. Consider the preceding verses: "Children, obey your parents in the Lord, for this is right. 'Honor your father and mother' (this is the first commandment with a promise), 'that it may go well with you and that you may live long in the land.' Fathers, do not provoke your children to anger, but bring them up in the discipline and instruction of the Lord" (Ephesians 6:1–4.)

The connection between the parent-child relationship and spiritual warfare is a strong one. When parents and children stop thinking of each other as the enemy and start to recognize who the real enemy is, a change in the relationship will begin. The powers of this dark world and the spiritual forces of evil hate a strong relationship between a child and a parent, so their goal is to break down all familial trust and goodwill.

Forgiven and Loved

Your job as a counselor will be to help Tim, Janet, and Maguire see that the life, death, and resurrection of Jesus changes their relationship. You will need to give them hope that they aren't alone in this struggle.

When counseling Maguire, one of the first things to learn is whether or not he is a believer. We know he enjoys youth group, but does he understand the gospel message? Does he believe that he is a sinner in need of a Savior? Does Maguire know he is a forgiven child of God? The good news of the gospel must be preeminent in every counseling session. Prayerfully share these gospel truths with Maguire. Ask the Holy Spirit to enliven his heart to all of the good news that is in the Word. Psalm 103 would be a beneficial place to start because the gospel is so clearly articulated in this chapter. He must be told that God forgives all his sins (v. 3). He must be told that God does not treat him as his sins deserve or repay him according to his iniquities (v. 10). He must be reminded that, "as far as the east is from the west, so far does he remove our transgressions" from him (v. 12). Children who are constantly being disciplined for bad behavior rarely hear that their sins are forgiven. This life-giving truth will turn Maguire's heart toward God instead of making him run further away. Like Adam and Eve in the garden when they were confronted with their sin, Maguire needs a covering, and God provides that for him in the death and resurrection of Jesus. The counselor should draw Maguire's attention to this good news.

Children not only need to hear that they are forgiven but that they are loved. Staying with Psalm 103 you can tell the child, "the LORD is merciful and gracious, slow to anger and abounding in steadfast love" (v. 8). If the child and parent are continually in conflict it will be good to hear that their heavenly Father is slow to anger and gracious and that he loves them. Because fathers are human, they will at times be quick to anger and very ungracious. Give the child hope that there is a perfect Father that loves them eternally. Verse 11 gives a very practical visual to help us remember how much he loves us. You could even take the child outside and ask them to look up and then read them this verse: "For as high as the heavens are above the earth, so great is his steadfast love toward those who fear him." Make sure the child understands that the word *fear* in this verse is not the same as the fear he feels when his parents are angry with him and he is not sure what is coming next; it is a holy reverence or a sense of awe.

The more that Maguire is aware of the forgiveness he has in Jesus, the more he will be able to forgive his parents when they fail him, and the freer he will be to ask for forgiveness from his parents when he sins against them. Point him to

Ephesians 4:31–32, "All bitterness, anger and wrath, shouting and slander must be removed from you, along with all malice. And be kind and compassionate to one another, forgiving one another, *just as God also forgave you in Christ*" (HCSB, emphasis mine). Ask him if he sees the correlation between being forgiven and not being someone given to arguing and anger. By the work of the Holy Spirit, the more he hears about his forgiveness, the more he will be able to put off the bitterness and anger described in verse 31 and practice the forgiveness described in verse 32. The power and the motivation to forgive and live in peace come from the forgiveness of God in Christ and the peace that has been offered to sinners from a holy God. Encourage Maguire to meditate on these truths by carefully reading through Ephesians 1:3–14, which describes at length our identity and heritage as followers of Jesus. As he reads, every time he sees "we" or "us," have him replace it with his name or "I". He needs to understand the truth that in love he was chosen to be adopted into God's family (v. 5), that in Jesus he has redemption and forgiveness of sin (v. 7), and he has obtained an eternal inheritance in Jesus (v. 11). You could also have Maguire go back to Psalm 103 and write out a list of the ways God demonstrates his love to him.

Given Approval and Identity

Children who are in constant conflict with their parents will either tend to think of themselves as a failure, a disappointment, or as one who is constantly misunderstood and persecuted. If they are focusing on their performance or the performance of their parents, they will end up depressed (caught in a sense of failure and disappointment) or pridefully angry (feeling completely misunderstood and persecuted). We most often see this played out when the child is constantly trying to win the approval of their parents. They will either end up dejected (depressed) or reject their parents in bitterness and pride.

Your goal as a counselor is to point children to the performance of Christ and what it has won for them, namely a new identity unconnected to their own performance. Help them see that in Christ, they are fully accepted and don't have to perform in order to have the Father's love.

In this counseling scenario, it would be helpful to take Maguire to 2 Corinthians 5:17, which tells him "Therefore, if anyone is in Christ, he is a new creation. The old things has passed away; behold, new things has come." Ask him about hurtful things in his relationship with his parents that he wants to forget. Ask him what it would look like for the dynamics with his parents to be improved. Remind him that he is new, that his identity is not wrapped up in the way he has acted in the past or the way his parents perceive him. His identity is new because of what Christ has done. The longer he is enslaved to his parent's opinion of him, the poorer their relationship will become. When children are constantly looking for the approval of their parents, they will feel like they never measure up and this will make them angry. Parents can sometimes have sinful and unrealistic expectations and often are too demanding of their children. Children often want to please their parents so that they feel good about themselves. They often think if their parents are happy with them then they must be right with God. But the truth is they are only right with God because of the work of Christ. If we show children that Christ has met all the demands God has for them, they will then be free to obey out of a different motivation. We want children to honor their parents out of gratefulness for what Christ has done for them, instead of what their parents will think of them.

Second Corinthians 5 goes on to talk about what this new identity and new way of thinking does in our lives. "Everything is from God, who reconciled us to Himself through Christ and gave us the ministry of reconciliation: That is, in Christ, God was reconciling the world to Himself, not counting their trespasses against them, and He has committed the message of reconciliation to us" (vv. 18–19, HCSB). Now that we are new, we have been given a new life and a new attitude. We have been reconciled or brought close. We no longer must fight for our own way, but instead we can fight for peace in our relationships. Maguire has been called to fight to love, his parents because Jesus has loved him. Ask him how he could walk out this calling on his life. Verse 19 gives him the motivation for wanting reconciliation—he is forgiven and he has been reconciled!

Maguire has been beat down by the compounded effect of his own sin and the sense of strife and unreasonable expectations from his parents. Giving him good news to lift his head and a good word to lift his heart will help him on the long road of changing behavioral patterns. Give him the truth of the gospel, followed by how he can live that out with his mom and dad. Help him see he doesn't need to fight for his rights because he is secure in all Jesus has given him.

A Word to Parents

Tom and Janet are both incredibly proud of what they have accomplished in life. They believe in earning a good reputation and a good life. What they don't realize is that this goal has superseded every other pursuit and shaped their relationship with their children. The strife in their home is largely a reflection of the lesser "gods" they are serving: achievement, success, and respect. Maguire's rebellion flies in the face of their primary belief that if you are good, good things will happen. They think they have been good parents, and they don't understand why Maguire can't just be a "good" kid—one who toes the line to meet their every expectation. They are blind to the unreasonable demands they place on their children, their idolatry of respect, and the fact that their desire to look good in the community outweighs their desire to love God and their son. They both think their anger at Maguire is justified because he acts argumentative and uncooperative. They harbor resentment toward their son and continually bring up his past mistakes.

Tim and Janet need to see the same truth about God's love, forgiveness, and acceptance that Maguire needs to understand. Ask them what they think God thinks of them—what his disposition is toward them. Take the parents to the parable of the unforgiving servant in Matthew 18:21–35. As you read these verses to them, ask them who they most identify with in the story. Ask them if they see themselves in the parable. Hopefully, by the work of the Holy Spirit, they will. At times each of us needs to be reminded of how much we have been forgiven. Tim and Janet need to hear Ephesians 2:8–9, "For you are saved by grace through faith, and this is not from yourselves; it is God's gift—not from works, so that no one can boast" (HCSB). The truth is that the best thing about them—their standing before God—is a gift, something they could never earn. Truly understanding this reality opens the door to reshaping their approach to parenting and understanding their goals as God's children.

Once Tim and Janet begin to see their hardness of heart toward Maguire, you can bring in the good news of the gospel. You may ask them if they see any sin in their own lives or in the way they interact with Maguire that might make it difficult for him to submit to their authority. Ask them if they think their speech and demeanor with Maguire is full of grace (Colossians 4:6). Ask them if they want to build up or tear down Maguire in the conversations they have with him. Ask them if they know why they get so angry when he is stubborn—is it because they are grieved that his heart is hard, or are they annoyed at the inconvenience he brings into their lives?

They might be afraid to hope that anything will change with their son. They might feel like their hearts have been broken too many times to ever want a deeper relationship with Maguire. Remind them that "The LORD is near to the brokenhearted and saves the crushed in spirit" (Psalm 34:18). There is hope for their relationship with Maguire. The greatest proof of that is how far God went to restore relationship with them and reconcile them to himself. Just as you told Maguire that he is forgiven and now has a ministry of reconciliation, help Tim and Janet see that pursuing reconciliation with their son is one of the primary ways they can express the love that Jesus has poured out on them. Have them look for ways to build Maguire up with their speech, instead of tearing him down (Colossians 4:6). Show them that healing in their relationship starts with repentance on their part. They must lead the charge in confessing their sin to Maguire and asking for forgiveness. This act alone is often exactly what the Holy Spirit uses to soften the hardest of hearts.

Take them to the same place you took Maguire, Ephesians 4:31–32. Have them make a list of their sins and next to each sin write the word *forgiven*. The more they are aware of how much they have been forgiven in Christ, the more they will feel the freedom to forgive. It will also give them the motivation to let their bitterness go. It will help them to be loving and kind toward Maguire and to see him not as an adversary, but as a brother in Christ.

Lastly, remind them that Maguire's performance does not reflect their identity. Their identity is now that of a loved and redeemed child of God. This identity isn't theirs because of their performance, but because of what Christ has done for them on their behalf. They both have been looking to Maguire and Sheila to make them feel good about their parenting. Sheila performed well and made them proud. Because Maguire hasn't performed to their standards, they are angry, depressed, and demanding. Be sure they know that their standing before God doesn't change based on the way their kids turn out. They have been living for the approval of society and themselves. Their relationship with Maguire is a failure, and that adds to their anger toward him. Instead, they need to believe the truth that they are forgiven and accepted, and because of that, seek to love Maguire the way they have been loved. Ask them to describe God's love toward them. Remind them that his love is a gift.

Have them memorize Ephesians 2:8–9, "For you are saved by grace through faith, and this is not from yourselves; it is God's gift—not from works, so that no one can boast" (HCSB). Have them recite this verse to each other and pray together that the Holy Spirit makes this joyous truth move their hearts to respond with gratitude. Ask them to be mindful of the times they boast about things they have accomplished. They need the joy of their salvation restored, or possibly they need to hear the good news of his precious gift for the first time.

There is hope for this family and others with these all-too-common relational tensions. Reconciliation is available to each of them through the finished work of Christ. God is in the business of turning the most difficult relationships into an opportunity to praise his glorious grace.

CHAPTER 6
HELPING A CHILD WITH FRIENDSHIPS
JONATHAN HOLMES

Brayden trudged up the driveway after the bus dropped him off from a long day at school. Jennie, his mother, waited on the porch and reached out to give him a welcome hug as he approached. Brayden tried to dodge her, and Jennie could tell by his puffy eyes that he had been crying. As she followed him into the house, she asked if something was wrong.

"I hate school. I don't have any friends, and no one likes me," he burst out.

"What do you mean?" Jennie asked. "You have a ton of friends! Everyone likes you!"

"No, I don't! No one likes me," he repeated. He slumped on the couch and curled up into a ball, hiding his face.

"Can you tell me why you feel that way?" Jennie sat next to him and put a hand on his shoulder.

"I don't want to talk about it," he said. "It's not a big deal anyways, and there's nothing you and Dad can do about it."

Jennie sat a while longer with Brayden and wondered to herself what might have caused all of this drama. While Brayden wasn't the most outgoing child ever, Jennie had always seen him as a friendly, warm, and compassionate kid who connected well with his peers. It broke her heart that he was struggling like this. She let the matter rest for the moment, telling him she cared deeply about his hurt and would see if he wanted to talk later.

Later that night, Jennie brought the situation up again, hoping Brayden might open up with his dad there. Even Brayden's older sister jumped into the mix, trying to figure out why he was saying he had no friends. Eventually, Brayden shared that a few weeks earlier a fellow classmate had teased him in front of other kids in the class. This embarrassed Brayden, and since then he'd been staying inside during recess and helping his teacher in the classroom.

Jennie and Mike asked if Brayden wanted them to talk to this boy's parents, and he quickly said, "No! That would make it even worse!"

Somewhat baffled, Mike and Jennie tried to find different ways over the next few weeks to draw Brayden out of his slump. They asked him if he wanted a friend to come spend the night. They tried to invite friends over from church on Sunday afternoon. They even thought about asking the school guidance counselor to talk to him. After more consideration, Mike and Jennie reach out to you for help.

Helping Children with Friendships

Brayden represents one of many children who struggle with friendships at school and in their community. Peer relationships represent a significant aspect of a child's life at home, school, church, and beyond. Friendships help children from the earliest stages of development to learn important social and relational skills and to form a sense of belonging in the world around them.

A child's struggle with friendships represents an understandable concern for parents, mentors, and educators. Developing and forging friendships at an early age is important because friendships and community help provide opportunities where children can learn to serve one another, look out for another person's interests, learn to ask questions, practice active listening, and offer encouragement. From cheering a friend on at a basketball game to helping a friend study for a tough exam, friends are indispensable for the journey of life. How can the counseling process help a child navigate and understand the ups and downs of his or her peer relationships? What skills may they need to develop or barriers might they need to overcome in order to develop healthy and meaningful rapport with the children around them?

Tell a compelling story about friendship.

One of the first steps in helping a child with his or her friendships is to communicate a compelling and biblical vision for what friendship is. Too often, friendship is seen as an optional social relationship—one which is disposable, replaceable, and not worth much effort. Biblical counselors can help by framing the story of the Bible as a story of friendship—using this simple outline:

1. You were made for friendship. [Creation]
2. Friendship has gone bad. [Fall]
3. Jesus redeems friendship. [Redemption]
4. Friends are friends forever. [Consummation]

Using the storyline of Scripture can be a helpful tool for the counselor to communicate the Bible's message of friendship. I would encourage a counselor to draw these four movements of friendship so the child can visualize and interpret them.

You were made for friendship.

God is the creator, and he made everything. He created friendship. Ask the child about their desire to have a friend.

- Tell me about one of the best friends you've ever had. What is he or she like?
- What do you want in a friend?
- Where do you think you got the desire to have friends?

Helping the child see that their draw and desire for friendship is good and rooted in God's design is essential to helping them understand the importance and priority of forming friendships.

Friendship has gone bad.

Unfortunately, the story of relationships—both the relationship between God and people and relationships between people—goes downhill in Genesis 3 on that fateful day when Eve succumbed to the serpent's temptation and ate the fruit. Share this story with your counselee, and together look to see how Adam and Eve first responded to God after they disobeyed his direct command.

They hid. They isolated themselves from God. Until this point, it was their habit to walk with God in the cool of the day, an expression of perfect friendship and community with him. Once they turned their back on God and sinned, however, their relationship with God was marred extensively, and they could no longer stand unashamed before him. Instead, they looked for ways to cover themselves and remain out of his sight. The damage that was done to Adam's and Eve's friendship with God then seeped into every other relationship on earth.

At this stage of the story, ask the child a few questions to help them understand the impact of the fall on their friendships:

- Have you ever been lonely? Have you felt left out at school or home?
- What is hard about your friendships?
- Is it difficult for you to build friendships? If so, why do you think that is so?
- Is it hard for you to get to know other kids? Do you feel shy or embarrassed around them?
- Has your friend done something that has hurt your feelings? Can you tell me a little bit about that?

These questions and the answers can help you show children that these same issues have affected friendships for a long time. They're not the first person to experience the difficulty of forming and keeping friendships. Indeed, many adults still struggle with these same issues in their own lives.

Jesus redeems friendship.

So what makes friendship good again? What can bring healing and restoration to our problem of being separated from God? As a biblical counselor, you can even help build anticipation by asking the child a question like this: Can you describe what you think the perfect friend would look like? After hearing his or her answer, you can affirm every great quality mentioned and follow up by asking, "Can I tell you about some qualities I'd be looking for in a perfect friend? Imagine a friend who knew everything about you and still loved you even when you weren't friendly. One who gave up his life for you. Can you imagine a friend like that? The apostle Paul tells us about a friend like that in Romans: 'but God shows his love for us in that while we were still sinners, Christ died for us.' (Romans 5:8)."

You can build on this conversation from there. "What good news! Jesus, the perfect friend, gives up his life for us so that we can be a part of his family. We are able to do friendship like the Bible calls us to because of this good news—because of the gospel. Because Jesus reached out to befriend us and to restore our relationship with him, he makes us new on the inside and puts his love for other people into our hearts, giving us his strength to reach out and love people around us."

Friends are friends forever.

Tell the child how the story gets even better from there. Not only does Jesus make friendship possible and good again, but now through Jesus Christ we can be friends forever. Not only is he the perfect friend, he's our forever friend. In John 15:13–15, Jesus is talking with his close friends the disciples, and he says,

> Greater love has no one than this, that someone lay down his life for his friends. You are my friends if you do what I command you. No longer do I call you servants, for the servant does not know what his master is doing; but

I have called you friends, for all that I have heard from
my Father I have made known to you.

You can elaborate in the following way: "What a sweet
truth from the lips of our Savior. No longer are we enemies
(Romans 5:10), we are called friends of Jesus! Jesus is our forever friend. He is always there, and will always be with us
(Hebrews 13:5). He is the ever-dependable, always-present,
ready-to-listen friend we have dreamed of. And for those who
trust and believe in him as their Savior, he will be their forever friend!" What good news this is for us and for the children we care for.

While friendships here on earth are difficult and hard
because of our sin and brokenness, it won't always be like
that. We can all look forward to a time when all of Jesus's
friends will unite together in heaven to worship him. Think
about this for a moment. Brainstorm out loud with your
counselee—what might perfected, Christ-centered friendships look like? No more fighting. No more bullying. No
more sitting at the lunch table by yourself. No more trying to
find recess buddies. No more friendship drama. Instead, you
will be joyfully worshipping God with all of your friends, and
those issues will be forgotten.

This story of friendship, embedded in God's Word, helps
the child understand that friendship is an important issue
God cares about. As a counselor you can then state two helpful observations to form the backbone of your counseling
time with the child:

1. Friendships are hard and often require sacrifice.
2. Friendships ultimately point to a greater Someone.

Friendships Are Hard and Often Require Sacrifice

Children often expect that friendships should be easy and fun. Children can have expectations that their friends think like them, talk like them, and enjoy the same things they do. Children often believe that friendship is ultimately about finding someone with similar interests as they have. Not only does this narrow down the pool of acceptable candidates for a child to socialize with, but it also teaches them that friendships should be easy and self-centered.

Jesus gives us the perfect example of friendship. There was nothing about us that deserved Jesus's friendship, and yet he drew near to us (John 1:14) and lived as one of us, taking the same risks in friendship that we take when we put ourselves in the vulnerable position of reaching out to see if someone wants to get to know us. He invested his time, attention, and care into a circle of disciples who were selfish, misinformed, and petty. He understands the challenges of being patient and persistent in seeking companionship. Yet he draws near to us, lays aside his own interests to be in friendship with us.

We must help children understand that friendship is a way that they mirror the storyline of Scripture. We can help teach and disciple our children that friendship is often hard and requires sacrifice and looking out for others' interests.

As it did for Brayden, our young boy at the beginning of the chapter, life brings hardship into friendship. I find that many of the issues children struggle with in childhood or adolescent friendships are quite similar to the struggles you and I have in adult friendships! Issues of rejection, fear, conflict, hurt feelings, unmet expectations, and embarrassment are present in both adult and childhood friendships. Helping the child learn and practice God's plan for friendship can help them as adults to navigate these inevitable waters.

Help children seek to resolve conflict with their friends in a biblical manner. Solving and working through problems is one of the most basic skills that friendship can teach a child. Help the child seek to understand and really get to know their friends. Help equip the child to ask good questions of their friends. Also equip the child for hard conversations when things go wrong in friendship and when misunderstandings occur.

A word on bullying and peer pressure in friendships

Bullying and peer pressure in friendships is a real thing. Unfortunately, there are kids at school who will use their words and actions to intimidate and incite fear in other kids. Social media and technology significantly magnify the issue. An individual can post something on any of the many social media apps, and it can be instantly seen and read by hundreds of kids.

Again, the Bible's storyline locates and explains why such things happen—sin has broken and fractured the way we behave as friends. While this doesn't do away with the pain of being bullied, it can remind the child that the bullying is not their fault. When helping children in situations where there is bullying and overt peer pressure toward bad behaviors, I try and equip children with the following truths (hand motions might be a way to remember them):

- *Pray up*: Remind the child that God is always with him or her. God shows up when people are being oppressed and hurt unjustly (cf. Genesis 16:13; Exodus 3:7–12). He cares about our friendships and what we go through. Encourage and bring comfort to the child by acknowledging that Jesus, their perfect Friend, knows what it is like to be bullied and made fun of (cf. Matthew 27:27–31). We can always turn to him in prayer.

- *Speak up*: How can the child diffuse some situations in the moment? Proverbs 15:1 explains, "A soft answer turns away wrath, but a harsh word stirs up anger." Work with the child to develop a list of wise replies that would be categorized as a "soft answer."
- *Shut up*: Proverbs 26:4 states, "Answer not a fool according to his folly, lest you be like him yourself." Help the child see that there are some situations where they need to close their mouth, pray to God for help, and walk away. This might mean they continue to get taunted, teased, and tested, but the fruitfulness of responding to the bully is lost at this point.
- *Go up*: Encourage the child to seek appropriate help when the bullying is chronic and cannot be resolved on their own. Talking to a trusted adult is not a sign of weakness or being a wimp, but showing and demonstrating wisdom.[1]

Friendships Ultimately Point to Someone Greater

Friendships are often hard and require sacrifice, and they ultimately point to a greater Someone. This, in my opinion, is a great missing element in our conversation when we counsel children about friendships. Friendships give children a practical and visible way to understand the gospel! What an exciting opportunity for children to be missionaries for the gospel—with friendships at home, school, and church.

Do children we counsel understand the weightiness of friendship? I venture that they do not. Again, our culture teaches almost the exact opposite when it comes to friendship. We are taught that *friendship is all about you! Find friends that enjoy the same things as you do! Friendship should be easy.*

This is important to communicate to our children. Friendships give them not only a picture of the gospel message, but also invite them to participate in the divine drama of redemption. Each time children move toward another friend, motivated by Someone and something greater than themselves, others are reminded of how God in Christ befriends them.

What easier way to talk to children about the gospel than through the lens and story of friendship? The following questions can help children see some of these concepts:

- List three or four of your friends. What do you like about them? What initially caused you to want to be friends with them?
- Do all your friends share the same interest? Are they all a similar age as you? Why do you think that is so?
- Should friendships be easy or hard? Why or why not?
- Have you ever considered being a friend to someone who is not like you? Why do you think that would be difficult—or why not?
- What's been the hardest thing for you to deal with in friendship? Does that make you want to pull away from the friendship?

- When things get hard in your friendship, how do you typically respond? Based on Jesus's example, how do you think he would respond?
- If people were to peek inside your friendships, do you think they would see the love of Jesus?

A Word to Parents

The principles above can function as a foundation and framework for you to build a theology of friendship for counseling children or discipling your own children. How you add to that framework will look differently for each family, but here are some helpful suggestions toward that end that I believe will encourage and foster good friendships with your children.

Model friendship yourself

If you want your children to have good friendships, ask yourself what kind of example you are setting for them. Do you and your spouse model the biblical friendship described above? Do they see a commitment to friendships that transcends common interests, stage of life, and shared hobbies? Do they ever see you move toward people who are unlike you in those ways?

As a family, my wife and I have sought to try (imperfectly!) to move toward people who are not exactly like us. We host people into our home who come from different backgrounds and stages of life. From cookbook clubs to game nights to deck nights, I want my children to see our family engaging in friendships at every level of life. The common thread that joins those together is our love for God, which then motivates us to love others in friendship.

CARING FOR THE SOULS OF CHILDREN

Help your child be a pursuer of friendship

I hear parents say, "No one wants to be my child's friend!" It's one of the most heartbreaking moments for us as parents. We want and hope that our children will have good friendships at home, school, and church. When those friendships don't materialize, it can be hurtful and painful.

We can help our children realize that they don't always need to be the one pursued, but they can be the pursuer! As we encourage our child to be an initiator in friendship, it helps reinforce the biblical message and gospel story. Here are some helpful ways to aid your child toward this end:

- Let's pray about one person in your class today that you can ask to sit with you at lunch or play with you at recess.
- Is there a friend you would like to invite to sit with us at church?
- Would you like to invite a friend over to the house to play?
- Is there anyone in your class who doesn't have a friend? Why do you think that is so? Do you think you could invite them into an activity or conversation?
- How would you want someone to come and befriend you? Why don't you try and do that this week with someone else!

Learn from your children when it comes to friendship

I learned something valuable about friendship from my daughter. A few years ago my two older daughters and I were at our local library. On this particular day, there was a sweet little girl in full leg braces with her walker in the corner near the activity area. My sweet and friendly daughter Ava immediately went over to introduce herself. In the space of seconds, she had asked the other girl her name (Hannah), what grade she was in (pre-K), and why she was in leg braces (unknown). As Hannah's mother kindly looked on, I nervously reordered the pile of books I had accumulated.

Then, as time went on and the girls happily became enveloped in their world of princesses, puzzles, and giggles, I relaxed and took a deep breath. There was no awkwardness now, just the fun whispers of girl-to-girl chatter.

As we walked out of the library, Ava looked up excitedly and said, "I can't believe I made a new friend!" In the coming weeks she would tell me she had seen Hannah at her school (they're a year apart) and had waved at her. Every once in a while, Hannah will come into our conversation, and Ava will remind me of the friend she met at the library that summer day.

Reflecting back, I'm so thankful for my daughter's kind heart and gracious outreach. Hannah's mom told me that day that not many kids reach out to her daughter because she has disabilities. In that moment, I realized how simple, yet profound, friendship can be in the life of a child. It can brighten one's day, put a smile on one's face, and in the best of ways, it can soften shame, alleviate stigma, and lift spirits.

That day my daughter taught me to enter into other people's worlds with love and care. You don't need to have fancy words or a planned-out monologue. Sometimes the simplicity of "Hello, I'm Ava" is all you need to begin a friendship.

Children and Their Emotions

CHAPTER 7
HELPING ANXIOUS CHILDREN[1]

JULIE LOWE

Chris is a sensitive ten-year-old boy from a loving family that is active in your church. He had very few experiences of prolonged stress or loss until his grandmother passed away during the summer. Shortly after that, his grandfather also passed away, along with a family pet. Chris began worrying about his parents' well-being (though they were perfectly healthy), and he became anxious about becoming ill or getting the flu. His parents became concerned when one day he refused to go to school because he knew several kids in his class had a virus. He wasn't willing to get on the school bus or even let his parents drive him to school. Chris's parents wondered if this was just a phase he was going through, a way of processing grief, or if he was developing a struggle that needed intervention. When he continued to refuse to ride the bus and go to school, they decided to seek outside help. They bring him to you for counseling.

What can you say to Chris to reassure him? How can you help Chris, and other children like him, to live at peace in frightening world? How can you help them find safety in an unsafe world?

As a counselor you are likely to encounter more and more children like Chris who are worried and afraid. Many families are seeing an increase in anxiety in their children. With mass media and a 24/7 news cycle, kids are continually exposed to the reality of global perils. News of epidemics, war, terrorist attacks, wildfires, internet hoaxes, and cyberbullying spread quickly. Children and adolescents are exposed more and more to frightening possibilities of calamity. There are also many sources of childhood fear and anxiety closer to home: the flu, germs, making mistakes, getting bad grades, peer ridicule, public speaking, not fitting in, the possibility of losing a loved one—the list goes on. For kids who have a disposition toward worry and anxiety, this exposure can have a snowball effect.

Paul Foxman, in his book *The Worried Child*, asserts that anxiety is the number one epidemic in the United States and that approximately 25 percent of the population struggle with it.[2] Foxman describes how we often give children conflicting messages that the world is both safe and unsafe. We walk into public schools with metal detectors and security guards. We talk about lining backpacks with protective metals. What message might that be giving children?

We go through airports with multiple security checks, pat-downs, and bomb-sniffing dogs, yet parents regularly tell their kids that they are safe and not to worry.

You've probably noticed that though several children are exposed to the same events, some struggle with anxiety more than others. Why might one child struggle more with anxiety than another child? There can be several factors. Every child is wired differently. They each have different strengths and weaknesses, and tendencies toward particular struggles or temptations. Some children have an innate temptation to wrestle with fear. They are more alert to potential risks and are in tune with the peril others are experiencing. This creates a heightened sense of vulnerability for them.

Chris's parents share with you that he has always been more cautious and worried than their other children. He is a perfectionist and always wants to get things right—finishing schoolwork, playing sports, even dressing. Some kids, like Chris, have personalities that are more perfectionistic, which can lead them to have difficulty relaxing, to be driven by the desire to please, to be non-assertive, and to avoid conflict. Kids like this often struggle with fear of people, including fear of disappointing or failing, and they may put high expectations on themselves. All of these tendencies lead to stress and anxiety.

Another cause of persistent anxiety in children may be prolonged exposure to stressful situations. Traumatic events, turmoil in the family, or an unpredictable lifestyle could lead to a sense of endangerment. The more we understand the cause of a child's anxiety, the greater success we will have in shepherding him or her through it, and the wiser and more practical we will be in speaking into their experiences. For Chris, it was clear that his anxiety centered on the loss of his grandparents.

As you assess an anxious child, how do you know when a child's fear is within "normal" range, or when is it problematic and needs intervention? From a counseling standpoint, you'd want to evaluate to what degree it is impeding their day-to-day life. How frequent is the fear/anxiety, how intense is it, and how long does it last? Is it preventing the child from engaging in daily activities? Is it impeding them from taking healthy risks and engaging socially? Perhaps the better question is, is their fear controlling them, or are they controlling their fear? Are they able to control/manage their anxiety, or does it control/manage them? At this point fear is controlling Chris. He is not able to function normally (i.e., attend school) without some kind of intervention from you and his parents.

When experiencing persistent anxiety, the tendency is for children to find comfort in controlling or shrinking their world to what feels manageable. Some children look for security or comfort in routine behaviors (such as thumb-sucking, sleeping with a parent, or performing other rituals), objects (television, books, or fantasy worlds), or people (a parent, sibling, or friend). Others avoid certain things (school, leaving the home, or getting in a car, bus, or plane because of fear). Chris was shrinking his world to where he felt safe—at home with his family.

Helping Chris Identify His Fears and Seek Shelter in God

Like most anxious children, Chris's fears were so visceral that it would not help him to just reassure him that he would be safe at school. He already knows that people do get sick at school, and he also knows that sometimes people die. For him, and for other anxious children, I often use this Boat and Refuge Activity.[3]

Boat and Refuge Activity

This activity provides a setting for anxious children to think about how their emotions and beliefs impact the way they look at life and where/how they find shelter. To do the activity you need 12 x 18 paper or larger and various art mediums—crayons, colored pencils, markers, etc.

Ask the young person to draw a boat—any boat they would like—and ask him or her to draw what type of surroundings the boat is in. Explain that they can draw whatever they'd like, and that there is no right or wrong way to do this exercise.

Follow-up questions and things to observe

After the child completes his or her picture, ask some of these questions:

- What type of boat did you draw, and why?
- Are you in the boat? Are you in the picture? Where?
- What else did you draw in the picture, and why?
- What type of body of water are you in? Why?
- Is the body of water calm or choppy or scary?
- What is the weather like? What season is it?
- Does anyone need to be rescued? If so, from what?
- How can help be given? And by whom?

Some children or teens will find this simply a fun activity but complete it so quickly and on such a surface level that you aren't able to gather much helpful information. For those children and teens, you can follow up by asking them to picture themselves and their life as a boat on the water. Ask them to redraw with this mind. But other young people will reveal a great deal about themselves and their views of safety, stability, how they find rest, and how they view the Lord. Here are some additional questions to ask:

- If God were to enter into this situation, what would he look like?
- How would he come?
- Consider the following passages from the Psalms. What are some ways God is described? How does this help you when you are facing a big storm in your life?
  - » Psalm 73:28: "But for me it is good to be near God; I have made the Lord God my refuge, that I may tell of all your works."

- » Psalm 62:7: "On God rests my salvation and my glory; my mighty rock, my refuge is God."
- What would it look like for God to be your refuge in this picture?
- What does it mean that the Lord is your rock?
  - » Psalm 18:2: "The Lord is my rock and my fortress and my deliverer, my God, my rock, in whom I take refuge, my shield, and the horn of my salvation, my stronghold."
- If God entered into this picture, what would you draw?
- How would he help?
- How would he be your deliverer? Your shield?

Brainstorm with the teen or child and see what they can come up with. Look for ways you can help make connections for them when they are struggling to do so themselves. Then consider how you can make those connections come to life in the actual places where they struggle. How can they trust God to be their deliverer, and what does that tangibly mean in their circumstances? What can and should they expect God to do or not do?

The Psalms are full of rich imagery for the ways God is their shield, protector, refuge, high tower, shelter, etc. Feel free to think winsomely and creatively for additional ways Scripture may speak to the child you are working with.

Pointing Children to Christ

As counselors, we can be tempted to reassure the anxious child we are meeting with that their fears are unfounded and that bad things won't happen. Sometimes that is the case, but most of the time I find that the children I counsel, like Chris, are afraid of genuine dangers and threats.

The truth is, just like adults, children live in a fallen, broken world where bad things happen. Cancer, danger, crime, and trauma are real. We all fail, make mistakes, get made fun of, and experience bullying. Life does not always turn out the way we would like it to. We have to be careful not to give a child false comfort or assurances we can't deliver. Your hope and theirs is found in the One who reigns over it all.

Whatever comfort we provide to children, we must ultimately point them to Christ who can meet them in the midst of their fear. As a counselor, my comfort is limited; it cannot guarantee or protect them from every fear. And my comfort is not always accessible. I cannot go to school with them, live inside their head, or be available every time they struggle. However, I can point them to the One who is always accessible, always available—whose comfort is perfect and limitless. "Fear not, for I am with you; be not dismayed, for I am your God. I will strengthen you, yes, I will help you, I will uphold you with My righteous right hand" (Isaiah 41:10 NKJV).

The Spirit can go places inside a child's heart and mind that you and I cannot. Our role is to reflect Christ by the comfort we provide to the children we talk with—and always leading them to him as their ultimate comfort. He can meet them in deeper and more meaningful ways than we ever can, and he also desires that they learn to depend on him in all of life's situations.

As I spoke with Chris, we read together 2 Corinthians 1:3–4 because it gives a picture of comfort that emulates Christ, "who comforts us in all our affliction, so that we may be able to comfort those who are in any affliction, with the comfort with which we ourselves are comforted by God." Here is this waterfall effect: You can provide comfort to a child because it has first been given to you. You can offer hope, because you have first found hope in Christ. As a counselor, you live out and embody before your children what Christ is and has done for you.

Chris and I talked about how God always offers his presence to his children in the midst of their fear. I shared with him that God reminds his fearful children over and over again that he is with them. Here are just a few of the verses I shared with Chris:

- When I am afraid, I put my trust in you. (Psalm 56:3)
- When my anxious thoughts multiply within me, Your consolations delight my soul. (Psalm 94:19 NASB)
- Even though I walk through the valley of the shadow of death, I will fear no evil, for you are with me; your rod and your staff, they comfort me. (Psalm 23:4)
- Be strong and courageous, do not be afraid or tremble at them, for the LORD your God is the one who goes with you. He will not fail you or forsake you. (Deuteronomy 31:6 NASB)

Children need to find hope and comfort in the right places. We don't want to guarantee that bad things won't happen, or offer false hope, or make promises we can't possibly fulfill. Young people often see through these thin attempts anyway. We *do* want to point them to the one (Christ) who can really meet them in their struggles and fears. Some kids need short-term help (accommodations, extra support, or comfort in the midst of a tragedy or hard experience). No matter the severity of their struggles, all apprehensive children need to know there is a God who walks with them through their fears. Wisdom is knowing what type of intervention they need, while wisely, consistently pointing them to greater faith.

For Chris, we made a plan that he would go back to school, with his parents driving him for the first week. Before he left the car, they would pray through Philippians 4:4–7 and remember together the comfort that the Lord is near and the promise that as they prayed the peace of Christ would guard his heart. We talked about him remembering to pray each time he felt anxious while he was at school. It was important to remind Chris that Jesus went with him when he got out of the car. The following week Chris's parents prayed with him before he got on the school bus and reminded him the Lord was with him—and they kept reminding him. Chris was able to go back to school, and the whole family learned to pray together about their day.

Thirteen Truths from Scripture to Comfort Anxious Children

As you foster an atmosphere of open conversation with the child you are helping, be sure to undergird your discussions with encouraging truths from Scripture. Here are some ideas to get you started:

1. You are not alone.

Psalm 23:4 (NIV): "Even though I walk through the darkest valley, I will fear no evil, for you are with me; your rod and your staff, they comfort me."

2. You have value.

1 Peter 2:9 (NIV): "But you are a chosen people, a royal priesthood, a holy nation, God's special possession, that

you may declare the praises of him who called you out of darkness into his wonderful light."

Matthew 10:31 (NIV): "So don't be afraid; you are worth more than many sparrows."

3. He sees your tears.
Revelation 21:4 (NKJV): "And God will wipe away every tear from their eyes; there shall be no more death, nor sorrow, nor crying. There shall be no more pain, for the former things have passed away."

4. There is help.
Psalm 46:1: "God is our refuge and strength, a very present help in trouble."

Hebrews 4:15–16 (NKJV): "For we do not have a High Priest who cannot sympathize with our weaknesses, but was in all points tempted as we are, yet without sin. Let us therefore come boldly to the throne of grace, that we may obtain mercy and find grace to help in time of need."

5. Your life has purpose.
Jeremiah 29:11: "For I know the plans I have for you, declares the LORD, plans for welfare and not for evil, to give you a future and a hope."

6. What you are going through is temporary.
2 Corinthians 4:16–18: "So we do not lose heart. Though our outer self is wasting away, our inner self is being renewed day by day. For this light momentary affliction is preparing for us an eternal weight of glory beyond all comparison, as we look not to the things that are seen but

to the things that are unseen. For the things that are seen are transient, but the things that are unseen are eternal."

7. There is a way out.

1 Corinthians 10:13: "No temptation has overtaken you that is not common to man. God is faithful, and he will not let you be tempted beyond your ability, but with the temptation he will also provide the way of escape, that you may be able to endure it."

8. You are more than the outward appearance.

1 Samuel 16:7 (NIV): "The LORD does not look at the things people look at. People look at the outward appearance, but the LORD looks at the heart."

9. You cannot imagine what good lies in store for you.

1 Corinthians 2:9 (NKJV): "Eye has not seen, nor ear heard, nor have entered into the heart of man the things which God has prepared for those who love Him."

10. You will not always feel this way.

2 Corinthians 4:8–9 (NKJV): "We are hard-pressed on every side, yet not crushed; we are perplexed, but not in despair; persecuted, but not forsaken; struck down, but not destroyed."

Psalm 30:5 (NKJV): "For His anger is but for a moment, His favor is for life; weeping may endure for a night, but joy comes in the morning."

11. You are greatly loved.

Jeremiah 31:3 (NIV): "I have loved you with an everlasting love; I have drawn you with unfailing kindness."

Ephesians 3:17–18 (NIV): "And I pray that you, being rooted and established in love, may have power, together with all the Lord's holy people, to grasp how wide and long and high and deep is the love of Christ."

12. You will not be put to shame.

Isaiah 54:4 (ISV): "Don't be afraid, because you won't be ashamed; don't fear shame, for you won't be humiliated—because you will forget the disgrace of your youth."

Hebrews 13:5–6 (NKJV): "Let your conduct be without covetousness; be content with such things as you have. For He Himself has said, 'I will never leave you nor forsake you.' So we may boldly say: 'The LORD is my helper; I will not fear. What can man do to me?'"

13. God is up to good in your life.

Genesis 50:20 (NIV): "You intended to harm me, but God intended it for good to accomplish what is now being done, the saving of many lives."

Romans 8:28 (NIV): "And we know that in all things God works for the good of those who love him, who have been called according to his purpose."

Reminding your child of unchanging promises from God's Word will give him or her a solid framework for processing worries and fears, both now and into adulthood.

Because we know that God's Word does not return empty (Isaiah 55:11), we can trust the Lord to root these truths deep into his or her heart and to bring them to mind when he or she needs them most.

Undergird all of your reassurances with reminders of who God is, who your child is in Christ, and the promises of the Lord's care and presence no matter what the circumstances are. This comfort is what your child needs most—not a promise that nothing scary or difficult will ever happen to them, but that the Lord of all creation is with them, is for them, and has a loving plan for their life.

A Word to Parents

When children are hurting, most parents agree that they would do anything to help provide relief. This means you might settle for solutions that bring short-term reprieve but can cause secondary problems.

Take, for example, six-year-old Monica, who is sincerely afraid of the dark. Each night at bedtime she begins her routine of checking under the bed and in the closet, as well as turning on night-lights and closing blinds. One night she sees something disturbing on TV. Though you've gone through her normal nighttime routine with her, she is still quite fearful. She looks panicked and is shedding tears, begging you to stay with her until she falls asleep. You've tried praying with her, playing soothing music, reading, adding a night-light, and giving her all versions of comfort you can think of. It is getting later, and you all are sleep-deprived. Eventually you give in and allow Monica to settle into bed with you so that you can all get a decent night's sleep. What started out as a survival tool for a rough season, however, slowly becomes the new normal. Monica likes the warmth and closeness of her parents and battles the idea of returning to her room.

Perhaps for another child, the coping mechanism you've settled on—allowing them to watch TV until they fall asleep—has become distracting. It began as a short-term solution in order to get them through a particularly challenging stretch of anxiety. Sometimes temporary decisions like these, made out of exasperation, quickly become permanent habits. Kids become dependent on the TV to fall asleep, on having a parent in the room, or another less-than-ideal comfort strategy that has been put in place. Kids don't start out depending on these methods, but they can become a secondary gain to being afraid. The child starts realizing, *I get to stay up late, watch TV, sleep with my parents, or* (fill in the blank). Children might not want to overcome their fears because it means losing something they have come to depend on or enjoy. What motivation will they have to overcome fear if it means losing a special privilege?

Do you see how, if we are not thoughtful and careful about how we approach our children's fears, we may unwittingly give them reasons to maintain them?

With constant media broadcasting every peril in the world, as well as more mature themes in shows that specifically target young people, the question remains, how do we infuse hope into a culture full of angst? Many shows and miniseries today entice young people either with darker themes or by portraying life as meaningless. In light of the many messages children are bombarded with, they need us to impart to them reasons that God is relevant to them. They need to find meaning and identity in things that genuinely fulfill. They need hope.

Have we given our kids reasons why they can live life fearlessly? Have we fostered conversations about hard topics and convinced them that no topic is too touchy for us to hear and no issue is off limits, that we can handle even the most intimate details of their lives with genuine love and concern? We must be proactive in fostering connections with our children. We must work tirelessly to engage them and invest deeply into their lives. This will powerfully counter any temptation for them to believe that what we offer is inconsequential or inadequate.

Let your child know they are not alone. Pursue meaningful conversation with your child. Be proactive in addressing hard topics they are bound to face in their world. Be a redemptive guide speaking into the corruption they will be forced to weed through. Let them know there is One who fights on their behalf.

CHAPTER 8
Helping Angry Children[1]

MICHAEL R. EMLET

Twelve-year-old Jacob is angry. Sometimes his anger is like an overcast day with the clouds scowling above, threatening rain and producing unease in those around him. Sometimes his anger is a prolonged rainstorm that nearly drowns everyone in the house. And sometimes his anger comes out of nowhere, like a late afternoon thunderstorm at the end of a predominantly sunny day. With that variability, part of the challenge for his parents is forecasting his emotional "weather" on a given day! Stay indoors or not? Bring an umbrella or not? Plan a picnic or not? His parents are deeply perplexed and discouraged, and so is he.

Jacob grew up in a strong Christian family and has two younger sisters. He professed faith in Jesus at a young age. His parents both work outside the home—his father full-time as an attorney for a Christian non-profit organization and his mother part-time at a local preschool. During the last year, his father has spent more time away from home traveling. Jacob is midway through the seventh grade, and the transition to middle school has been challenging. Although he was always near the top of his class in elementary school, he has struggled with the new workload in middle school. Furthermore, his two best friends moved away last summer and he still doesn't have deep friendships either at school or in his small church youth group.

Jacob describes himself as "feeling things deeply." His parents would concur. As a younger child he was generally very happy but seemed to have a low threshold for frustration and outright anger. This has only intensified with the challenges and changes of the last couple of years. Jacob says, "Sometimes I don't even know why I'm so angry. Some days I just feel constant irritation with everyone around me. Other times rage just wells up within me and I can't seem to stop it. I say things I don't really mean that hurt my sisters or my parents. We work it out later and ask for forgiveness, but I still feel guilty."

On the worst days anger envelops the entire family, escalating into yelling and harsh words particularly between his parents and himself. Once Jacob was so angry he threw his metal water bottle against the wall, crushing the bottle and knocking the plaster off the wall. Several times he left the house while enraged, slamming the door, walking to a nearby park, and ignoring frantic texts from his parents as to his whereabouts. His parents, too, have lost their temper, particularly his father. Sometimes his parents have responded in punitive ways, angrily taking away privileges like Jacob's phone or Xbox without really talking about or processing what happened. They walk on eggshells, afraid at any moment that Jacob will erupt in anger over something minor.

Finally they come to you for help, asking, "Can there ever be real peace in our home, or are bickering and outright fighting going to be the norm?"

When anger has become a pattern in a child's life, how can you help? You know that "human anger does not produce the righteousness God desires," but how can you minister to a child in such a way that he learns to be "quick to listen, slow to speak, and slow to become angry" (James 1:19–20 NLT)?

Where Does Anger Come From?

Like all of our emotions, anger does not come out of nowhere (although it sometimes seems like it does). Emotions don't just happen *to* a child; they are what the child *does* or *experiences* as an expression of his heart before God. In other words, our emotions are tied to our hearts, our inner nature that either is living for God or against God in every moment. What is in our heart toward God directly affects our emotions, our words, and our actions. Notice what God says about the way our hearts are connected to everything we think, feel, say, or do:

- "A good man brings good things out of the good stored up in his heart, and the evil man brings evil things out of the evil stored up in his heart. For the mouth speaks what the heart is full of." (Luke 6:45 NIV)
- "For out of the heart come evil thoughts—murder, adultery, sexual immorality, theft, false testimony, slander." (Matthew 15:19 NIV)
- "The acts of the flesh [i.e., actions flowing from a heart set against God] are obvious: sexual immorality, impurity and debauchery; idolatry and witchcraft; hatred, discord, jealousy, fits of rage, selfish ambition, dissensions, factions and envy; drunkenness, orgies, and the like." (Galatians 5:19–21 NIV)
- "You have heard that it was said to the people long ago, 'You shall not murder, and anyone who murders will be subject to judgment.' But I tell you that

anyone who is angry with his brother or sister will be subject to judgment." (Matthew 5:21–22 NIV). Notice that Jesus puts murder and anger in the same category—with the same punishment—because both issue from the heart.

The Bible's emphasis on the inward origin of anger suggests that helping angry children involves more than developing mere anger management techniques. To solve a child's anger problem, you must target the source of his anger—his heart.

Of course, not all anger is wrong. God's anger is holy, just, and loving, both in motive and expression. For Christians, it's appropriate and even necessary to experience anger about the injustices and sins that rightfully anger God. It's possible to experience anger and not sin (Psalm 4:4; Ephesians 4:26), but most likely, our anger is not honoring to God the majority of the time, either in its heart orientation ("I want what I want and you can't stop me") or its expression (rage, disrespectful speech, throwing objects).

Knowing that Jacob's anger comes from his heart should fill you—and him—with hope. He is not a slave of his passions and incapable of change. Jesus lived, died, and rose again so that all kinds of people, including children (and parents!) with very angry hearts, could be changed into people who love God and others.

Aim for the Heart

Since the child's heart is the source of his anger, helping him overcome anger involves targeting the root cause. Often children and teens will resist seeing temper outbursts as originating from their own hearts. They will want to blame parents, siblings, or circumstances for their sullenness or rage. But the child needs to learn that he is responsible for his anger. No one causes another person to sin; outward behavioral eruptions are caused by inward (heart-based) desires (James 1:13–15). At the same time, Scripture also teaches that "a harsh word stirs up anger" (Proverbs 15:1 NIV) and exhorts fathers not to "provoke" their children (Ephesians 6:4). These "provocative" factors have to be considered as well in the total picture of a struggling child, and we'll look at those later.

One goal in working with children and adolescents is to help them understand how their anger operates directly against God. Remember that the goal is not "nice" children who say "Yes ma'am" and "No sir," but children who understand that they live under the ultimate authority of God. Too often parents (and sometimes counselors) only focus on the "horizontal" aspect of the child's sinful behavior—what the child has done to disrupt human relationships. Targeting the heart helps children understand that their angry attitudes, words, and actions disrupt relationship with God, first and foremost. This Godward focus actually keeps the gospel front and center, because sin against God and others has a remedy! If we confess our sins honestly, he is faithful and just to forgive us and cleanse us (1 John 1:9).

Targeting the heart also involves understanding the reasons behind angry outbursts. It's not as simple as, "Jacob's a sinner and he wants his own way!" That's a general truth about all human beings, but it is not particularly helpful in the moment. Rather, you need to uncover the particulars of *this* child's "own way." Ask God to guide you by his Spirit so that you will have the biblical wisdom to grasp what is really going on in your counselee's heart when he is angry.

Anger generally reflects much more than simple frustration over blocked, self-oriented goals. Often it is a final common pathway of other emotions and experiences such as fear, shame, guilt, grief, disappointment, and loneliness. Anger is experienced by others as a dangerous and prickly porcupine, but many times, anger has a "softer" underbelly of hurt that is critical to explore in the life of your young counselee. In other words, angry children are not only inflicting suffering on others; they are often suffering intensely themselves in ways that are important to uncover. In light of this, consider questions such as the following:

- What specifically does this child desire, want, fear, or believe in the moments of anger? Or on a day when they simply feel cranky and "off"? Some older children may be self-aware enough to answer questions like these outright. But often you will have to play the role of a detective.

- Do you see any evidence for contributors such as shame, guilt, sadness, grief, loneliness, discouragement or depression that may underlie the anger?

- Concurrently consider what God says that speaks to these desires, motives, fears, and other emotional experiences. Consider his character, promises, actions, consolations, and commands. Remember God's goal in uncovering his people's hearts is restorative, not punitive. He longs to rescue wayward hearts and console hurting hearts.

CARING FOR THE SOULS OF CHILDREN

The answers to these questions will help you craft a wise and winsome, heart-oriented counseling approach. As children grow to understand how their desires, fears, and beliefs fuel their destructive anger, you can point them to Jesus for specific help. He promises to pour out grace and mercy in time of need—I'll give some specific examples later in this chapter.

Understand the Wider Context of Anger

Along with understanding the desires, fears, and motives of a child's heart, it is also very important to discern the potential physical and circumstantial factors that might contribute to a child's struggle with anger. While it is true that anger ultimately stems from the heart, it is crucial to ask what other contributing factors may be present. Considering the heart gives a *deeper* understanding of anger problems; considering the situational factors gives a *wider* understanding.[2] Understanding the wider context of your counselees' lives will help you be more patient, compassionate, and creative as you work with them. Discerning these various facets of a child's struggle requires wise, patient questioning and good listening.

Certainly, there may be temperamental dispositions toward anger. We are each created with certain strengths and weaknesses. This does not excuse sinful manifestations in all these areas, but it does remind us that just because we don't struggle as intensively with a particular pattern doesn't mean we are better than the other person. A naturally even-keeled parent or counselor needs to be careful of having a judgmental or impatient attitude toward the one who struggles with anger.

Regarding potential physiological factors, research has demonstrated certain characteristics are typical of children who tend toward explosive anger.[3]

- Difficulties with short-term memory
- Decreased ability to organize and plan
- Difficulty with multitasking
- Being a "black-and-white" thinker (i.e., rigidity in problem solving—"There's only one way to do this"—rather than flexibility—"There are several ways to approach this problem")
- Problems shifting quickly from one situation or set of expectations to another
- Difficulty in expressing oneself verbally
- Weaknesses in social skills (e.g., difficulty recognizing nonverbal cues; difficulty understanding how one is coming across to another person)

Notice these potential weaknesses are *not* sin issues. They may *predispose* the child you're working with to respond in an angry, explosive way if he or she is challenged, but they are not sins in and of themselves. However, when these weaknesses are present, the temptation increases for the child to become frustrated and lose control. How might the presence of some of these factors impact how you help parents shepherd their children?

Here's one scenario that the parents of your counselee may face. When their child explodes in response to their request, "Please clean up your room before dinner," what's going on? While it's true that heart issues of laziness and love of comfort may be motivating the disobedience, perhaps the child is struggling to prioritize an approach to the mess, which may lead more quickly to frustration. Have parents break the task into bite-size pieces: "First, pick up your shoes and put them in the closet. Okay, good. Now pick up your books and place them back on the shelves." Their child may still struggle to obey, but they have made appropriate allowance for his or her potential weaknesses.

Additionally, if a child doesn't seem to shift easily from one situation to another, plan accordingly. Parents may still require him to turn off his device a few minutes before dinner, but giving ten-minute and five-minute warnings may go a long way in preventing a blowup when the time actually comes to press the "Off" button.

Finally, if you learn that your counselee has been the victim of teasing or bullying at school, this too will factor into your overall approach to the anger that occurs at home after school. It doesn't excuse your child's anger, but it does flesh out the broader contours of the struggle. God always considers a suffering person's context even as he provides a remedy for sinful responses.

So, in order to minister with depth and breadth to the child you are coming alongside, maximize your understanding of the various facets of his or her struggle (heart, body, and situational) and adjust your approach accordingly. What might this look like more specifically?

A recent blowup between Jacob and his parents happened one afternoon when his parents asked him to take out the trash several times over the course of two hours. He kept saying he would, but he didn't. He lay on his bed, listening to music. His exasperated parents stepped up their demand with a threat—"Do it now or you can't go to the basketball game tonight!" Jacob angrily stormed out of his room, slamming the door and knocking some paint off the doorframe. "All you do is nag me. One demand after another! Can't I get a little downtime after school before becoming your slave?!"

This *seems* like a simple case of not wanting to be disturbed in order to do something unpleasant. Perhaps you could imagine a scenario in which laziness *is* the driving heart issue—he just doesn't want to trouble himself to get out of bed to do something he finds distasteful. But not this time. As you and Jacob talk, he describes an experience during gym class earlier that day when he came in dead last during a 400-meter run. Some of his more athletic classmates teased him, laughing about how hard he was panting.

"It just confirmed how out of place I feel in this school. I feel like a loser. No one understands how lonely it is. I felt really down and just wanted to listen to some music that would help calm my mind. It was working until my parents kept insisting I take out the trash." This gives a much fuller picture of Jacob's anger. He is not only a sinner; he is a sufferer. He is struggling with shame. He feels discouraged and alone. But the primary way it came out was destructive anger. God speaks into each of these experiences. Jacob tells a story of shame, isolation, and powerlessness. God tells a story of shame covered, isolation banished by communion with him and other believers, and powerlessness overturned by the indwelling of the Spirit.

No one place in Scripture fully captures Jacob's experience, but certainly Psalm 25 connects in a number of ways. It models for him how to turn to God in his distress at any point in the unfolding struggle, from his humiliation on the track to the wrath unleashed on his parents.

In the midst of being teased and ridiculed, Jacob can cry out:

To you, O LORD, I lift up my soul.
O my God, in you I trust;
   let me not be put to shame;
   let not my enemies exult over me. (v. 2)

God understands his sense of isolation and loneliness:

Turn to me and be gracious to me,
   for I am lonely and afflicted. (v. 16)

Jacob can appeal to God's companionship even as he prays for God to provide better friendships at his middle school:

The friendship of the LORD is for those who fear him,
   and he makes known to them his covenant. (v. 14)

And when he has displayed ungodly anger and feels an acute sense of failure, this psalm gives him words to return to the Lover of his soul:

Remember not the sins of my youth or my transgressions;
   according to your steadfast love remember me,
   for the sake of your goodness, O Lord! (v. 7)

Consider my affliction and my trouble,
   and forgive all my sins. (v. 18)

Jacob wouldn't use these exact words, of course. You want him to make the psalmist's words his own, amplifying where appropriate. For example, he might pray, "You promise that the soul of 'the man who fears the LORD' will 'abide in well-being' [25:12–13]. God, I want to honor you, but my life

Helping Angry Children

doesn't feel like 'well-being' to me. My dad is away too much. I've lost my best friends. I'm struggling to keep my grades up. I need help!" Listening to him pray also gives additional inroads for meaningful conversation (e.g., his dad's absence, his academic struggles).

As Jacob's counselor, you are modeling the grace and mercy of Jesus Christ to him. You want him to experience that Jesus *gets* him and is *with* him. As he is able to dig beneath the outward manifestations of his anger, seeing that he has a very busy heart indeed, you want to help him express what he is learning with his parents. They may well be in the dark concerning the complex mix of sadness, shame, and sinful desires at work in Jacob's life.

Sometimes in bringing Scripture to bear on a child's anger, we tend to focus solely on passages that speak about ungodly anger and its folly (e.g., Proverbs 14:29; 29:22; Ephesians 4:26–27; James 1:19–20). No doubt these biblical perspectives are important to discuss. But recognizing that anger has broad and deep roots helps you as a counselor to minister the good news of Jesus just as broadly and deeply. For example, talking about the fact that God himself displays righteous anger toward those who perpetrate injustice and oppression can help Jacob entrust himself to the One who judges justly (Psalm 10; 1 Peter 2:23).

Interaction with Jacob over these blessed truths is likely to take multiple meetings, and you will no doubt face resistance at points. But as he experiences Jesus meeting him in his places of weakness and pain, empowering him to respond honestly without sinful anger, and forgiving him when he does fail, hope for change will begin to build. Of course, with younger children who struggle with anger, you need to be

121

more concrete, breaking up biblical truth into bite-size pieces and potentially incorporating art, music, and toys into the interaction. The way you express these truths from Scripture needs to be developmentally appropriate (see chapter 3 for more information on stages of development).

A Word to Parents

It's inevitable that as parents, you get caught in the cross fire of your child's anger. More than you may want to admit, you contribute to the firefight by displaying impatience, harshness, anger, or withdrawal, which only exacerbates the problem. This is a place where you are likely to become disheartened and hopeless, not only about your child's struggle, but also about your own sinful expressions of anger. It's easy to become so focused on the problem that you miss opportunities to see God's grace in action. Let me suggest three overall ways in which you can influence the "weather patterns" in your home: (1) proactively strengthening your relationship with your child, (2) modeling consistency, simplicity, and dependency, and (3) developing a plan for the crisis moments.

First, proactively strengthen your relationship.

The focus here is on relationship building with your child as opposed to problem solving in the moment. To use a medical analogy, a healthy diet and exercise are protective against heart disease. Doing those things may not fully protect a person against a heart attack, but diet and exercise go a long way in preventing such a problem. Similarly, concentrating on building relational bonds with your child has preventative value. Here are some practical relationship building tips:

- *Look for ways to accentuate your child's strengths.* Don't focus so much on the weakness and sin that you can't see the ways God has uniquely gifted your child and is at work in her life (1 Corinthians 12:7).
- *Look for opportunities to enjoy your difficult child.* Too often, the sum total of your interactions with your child can feel negative. Seek to create times of pure enjoyment together. Show physical affection. Devote quantity time (not simply quality time) to engaging with your child in their interests. If your child does not believe that you love and enjoy her because you don't express it, you've got a strike against you when conflict brews.
- *Examine the way you speak about your child to others.* Does it border on slander? Or do you season your conversation with thankfulness about the good you see God doing with your child (Ephesians 4:29)? When you practice identifying the good in your child before others, it softens your own heart and positively affects your interactions with her.
- *Look for ways to say yes to your child's requests.* Too often we say no out of our own desire for convenience or comfort. God is a Father who lavishes good gifts on his children (Romans 8:32). As an exercise this week, make a mental note of the balance between the times you say no to your child versus yes. You may be surprised—and convicted!
- *Seek to understand the deeper and wider contributors to your child's anger.* As I noted above in Jacob's case, it is important to carefully and lovingly probe beneath the surface of your child's angry behaviors. This

communicates that you care about the totality of your child's experience, not just keeping her in line.

- *Pray!* Heartfelt prayer is a sign of humble dependence on God and hopefulness that God is and will be at work in the life of your child. Examine the content of your prayers for your angry child. Are they full of your own repentance? Are they full of character-oriented petitions for your child, like praying specifically for the fruit of the Spirit in her life (Galatians 5:22–23)? Ask God to give you wisdom to address heart, body, and circumstantial aspects of your child's struggle.

Second, model consistency, simplicity and dependency.

- *Consistency.* Model consistency by practicing what you preach. If you habitually express the wrong kind of anger in your tone, words, or actions, your child will resent being held to standards you don't keep. Also, model consistency in expectations and rules. Be clear about what you expect from your child, not changing your expectations from one day to another. Lastly, model consistency in discipline. You should have a plan for how you will respond to your child's misbehavior. Don't treat every offense as a "10" on a scale of 1–10. When your child is out of control, it's easy to simply react and discipline out of frustration. When you do that, discipline is often punitive, not restorative.
- *Simplicity.* Model simplicity by giving your child simple and clear instructions. Overloading him with instruction or explanation might precipitate a meltdown and will surely make a tantrum in progress

worse. "Too much talk leads to sin. Be sensible and keep your mouth shut" (Proverbs 10:19 NLT).

- *Dependency.* Model dependency on God by repenting in front of your child when you haven't been consistent or simple, or when your own anger makes things far worse. Failure becomes an opportunity for restoration and relationship building. When you sin against your child, go to him and explicitly confess your sin (James 5:16; 1 John 1:9). Ask him to pray for you, that God would help you to be a more faithful, Christ-honoring parent, showing your child that you also must depend on God to help change your own heart and behavior.

Third, develop strategies for crisis moments.

You need to have a plan for helping your child when she is tempted to lose control. Most parents only have two options in their response toolbox: sticking to their expectations for obedience right now (which usually leads to a tantrum) *or* dropping or reducing their expectations (which usually keeps the peace). While either option may in fact be a wise and godly choice in certain situations with the right parental motives and tone, other approaches may be more helpful with children struggling consistently with anger. Here are some options you can add to your response toolbox:

- *Pause.* Give your child time alone so she can regain self-control. This is not the same as a time-out, where you isolate a child for a set period of time as an act of discipline. Instead, this is a time for your child to calm down and reconsider her defiant attitude.[4] The pause can also help you to cool down, keep you from disciplining impulsively, and prayerfully think through your interaction with your child. When your child regains control, remember to affirm her. In the parable of the two sons (Matthew 21:28–32), notice how Jesus commends the son who initially refused to obey but later did what his father asked.

- *Use humor or laughter.* Sometimes a smile, a hug, or a tickle disarms your child, de-escalates a brewing battle, and allows you and your child to regroup to address the issue at hand. Consider this a "gentle response" that turns away wrath (Proverbs 15:1).
- *Cooperate creatively.* Work with your child to come up with a solution that takes both of your concerns seriously and is God-honoring and mutually acceptable. Although this *can* work in the heat of the moment, it is better to practice this proactively during a calm time, particularly if there are typical situations that set off your child's anger.

Let's say a typical flash point for you and your daughter occurs about thirty minutes before dinner when she complains of hunger and asks for a snack. You don't permit a snack that close to dinnertime because you're afraid she will spoil her appetite. Creative cooperation begins with you and your child understanding each other's desires and concerns (Philippians 2:4). Your daughter's concern is hunger. Your concern is that she might spoil her appetite for the good meal you're making. Notice that neither desire is sinful. The next step is to work together to find a solution that addresses both concerns. What does a conversation that moves toward creative cooperation sound like?

Perhaps earlier in the day you could ask your daughter why she often wants to eat a snack right before dinner. When she responds that she's usually really hungry by then, you can acknowledge that it is hard to wait the additional time until dinner, thereby affirming her. You can go on to simply express your concern that if she eats a snack too close to mealtime she won't have room for a good meal. Ask her if the two of you can work together to solve this problem in a way that honors God. This is a critical moment where you can encourage your child to be part of a mutual solution, rather than simply imposing a solution on her. She might respond with the idea that in such a situation she could grab a small handful of peanuts or a piece of cheese instead of something bigger that would spoil her appetite. You might agree to try this for a week to see how things go. Other mutually satisfying solutions could be packing her a larger lunch or planning an earlier dinnertime.

Of course, this is an easy case. Many other times it won't be that simple, and you will also have to proactively address the underlying heart issues that motivate defiance and anger as I've noted throughout this chapter. Even if your daughter is hungry, that doesn't give her license to fly into a rage. At the same time, working toward a mutually satisfying, God-honoring solution will go a long way to prevent future outbursts.

To conclude, let me remind you of Paul's words in Romans 5:20, "But where sin increased, grace abounded all the more." This is true for your child and for you. You will both fail repeatedly. But when *you* are experiencing the abounding grace and forgiveness of Jesus in the midst of your parenting failures, you are emboldened to press on in ministry to your struggling son or daughter. And be assured that because Jesus is a faithful high priest who sympathizes with your weaknesses, he will continue to pour out his grace, mercy, and wisdom as you seek him (Hebrews 4:15–16) so that you might be an instrument of redemption in the life of your angry child.

CHAPTER 9
COUNSELING AFTER A SUICIDE ATTEMPT
GARRETT HIGBEE

Mariah was fifteen years old and a sophomore in high school when she attempted suicide. She was a good student, an athlete, and had lots of friends. It devastated her parents and shocked all but her closest friends. Most didn't know that she was living in private despair. There were small signs, but nothing obvious that would have suggested the depth of her suffering. How did her hopelessness get this extreme? What led to such a desperate act?

Mariah grew up in a Christian home with a loving father, a caring mother, and two younger siblings. Other than typical family disagreements, they got along well. When she was younger, her parents sometimes yelled behind closed doors and seemed cold and distant for awhile, but they always got over it. She did worry that her parents might divorce. As she grew older, she was closer to her dad. He "got her" and listened better than her mom. She loved her mom and wanted to be closer, but her mother seemed preoccupied with taking care of everyone else.

Mariah desperately wanted to be liked. She thought the girls in the popular crowd weren't too nice, but sometimes she joined in with them on social media and made fun of less popular girls. She always felt bad about it later. She was becoming a good volleyball player, but also felt the pressure not to let her team down. She feared getting a C in math for the first time. She also found out her best friend was moving. All of this added to her stress. She was feeling increasingly insecure. She worried that no one liked her and that she couldn't keep up with the expectations of her parents, teachers, coaches, and peers. Classes were harder, boys seemed ruder, and girls seemed pettier.

To some degree, church was a refuge. She liked her youth group and was close to one youth leader, but she still felt a need to look her best when at church. Mariah shared some of her fears with a small group at church. They were sympathetic, but no one really followed up to learn more or give her counsel. She always seemed pretty together, and the culture at her church was to look good and trust God.

She grew increasingly isolated mentally and emotionally. She even found herself pulling away from Katie, the best friend who was moving. She reasoned that pulling away now would make it easier when Katie left. Around this time, Mariah started to have self-condemning thoughts. Things like, *You'll never be good enough. You're not as pretty as them or as smart as her.* She had posted a few things on social media about her faith, and while some affirmed her, others made fun of her at school. She only heard the critics getting louder and louder and often cried when she was alone. She tried alcohol a few times. She would have taken the pills others offered her at parties, but she had promised her coach and team she would not do drugs.

Her mom grew more concerned when she heard her crying at night, so she looked at Mariah's phone. She was shocked at Mariah's browsing history and posts. It seemed like she was becoming someone else. When her parents tried to talk about their concerns, Mariah became angry and felt her parents had violated her privacy. She went even deeper into her shell, showing less and less interest in her friends, volleyball, and time with family. The rest of the summer was tense. Her parents increased rules and restrictions. As the new school year approached, Mariah's parents forced her to see a counselor recommended by her school. Mariah reluctantly went, admitted to being depressed, but did not disclose much. After several sessions, the counselor referred her to a psychiatrist, who prescribed an antidepressant.

At first the medicine did not seem to have much effect. Over time, Mariah reported that it made her feel weird—she had more energy, but also was increasingly agitated. She felt like she had no escape from the pressures and stresses in her life and yet was obsessed with wanting out. One of her friends confided in her that she was cutting and that it brought a strange sense of relief. Mariah tried superficial cutting, but it did not have the effect her friend described.

Mariah became more defiant and distant at home. Her parents did not know what to do. When they reached out to the counselor, they were told to be patient while the meds kicked in. They were told to let her know they cared and to give her space. Mariah was angry, lonely, felt deeply misunderstood, and under tremendous pressure to be someone she did not know how to be.

One Sunday morning her parents permitted her to stay home from church. Sitting alone, she felt like it would be better for everyone (including her family) if she was gone. She went to her parents' medicine cabinet and swallowed her mother's sleeping pills with two glasses of wine.

When her family got home from church, her mother found her passed out in her bed. They called 9-1-1, and within minutes she was in an ambulance heading for the hospital. When she came to, she was confused, embarrassed, and fearful. Then the pastor showed up, and she realized that her issues were out in the open. The pastor prayed with the family and took the parents aside to suggest getting biblical counseling at the church. The parents hadn't even considered this option.

Preparing to Counsel Mariah and Her Parents

Historically, biblical counseling has affirmed that the best way to counsel a child is through good parental counseling. I believe this is wise. I've found that in complicated situations like this, however, the best counsel for children is most often a combination of working with the child and the parents— sometimes together and sometimes independently. Generally, the younger the child the more parental involvement is needed. While I believe parents need to be an active part of a teen's life and even have a part in the counseling, it is also important to allow the teen to have some autonomy and confidence that things said to the counselor will be kept private (unless life threatening). Coaching the parents through this ordeal while counseling their daughter can be done by the same counselors, but having a soul care team come alongside is ideal. In our case that would include a counselor and advocate (mentor) for Mariah and a counselor and advocates for the parents. We would work together as a team, providing proper care for Mariah while not neglecting the parents.

Before You Start

Here are some issues to be aware of and to address before you begin counseling:

1. When counseling teenagers, make provisions for context and confidentiality right from the start. Talk to the teen's parents about what is appropriate to share and what might not be. Assure them that you will keep them informed of any life-threatening, life-altering issues that might arise. Explain to them why it is important for their teen to have someone to talk to who will keep other matters confidential.

2. As a male counselor, I always have a woman in the room (apprentice, advocate for Mariah, or female co-counsel) when I counsel a female.

3. Remember that teens often struggle in formal counseling relationships. It seems forced to them, and usually it is initiated by parents who are motivated to find someone to help their child. Most teens don't share that level of motivation, especially if they see the counselor as a proxy to their parents. How do we get past these somewhat daunting realities to connect to Mariah personally? One way would be to assign another counselor to the parents, so they are getting biblical help from a counselor other than their child's counselor. Another option would be meeting with them separately to coach them regarding how to heal and care in the aftermath of this crisis.

Counseling Mariah

Mariah felt so alone. She felt that few other girls struggled like her. In fact, her temptation and struggles are not rare, and it is helpful to remind her that she is not a freak (1 Corinthians 10:13). Teenage suicide is the third highest cause of death for her age group. Girls contemplate suicide more than boys and attempt at a higher rate as well.[1] While teenage boys are less likely to attempt, they are more likely to be successful when they do. Teenage suicide is a growing issue in the United States. So how can we help? Let's begin by looking at how to approach counsel with Mariah.

Approach Mariah as a Sufferer

We need to connect with Mariah (and any other teen), before we can correct. She is depressed, anxious, and in biblical terms "fainthearted." When someone is suffering, we need to start by showing compassion. Mariah already knows she has been difficult; she knows she should have talked to her parents more. She knows she acted desperately and could have found better ways to handle her life. These issues will need to be addressed at some point, but now it is important for her to understand that God kept her safe even through her desperation. She needs to hear how much she is loved, not how disappointed her parents are. We need to counter the lies she has been telling herself with the truth of God's love and care for her. She needs to be reminded of the gospel and how God is near the brokenhearted and wants to draw near to her. She needs to be reminded that trusting in God is her real hope to overcome loss, loneliness, fear of man, and fear of failure. As I counsel Mariah and her parents, I follow a simple but effective method for counseling called the CARE model. "CARE" stands for connect, assess, respond, and encourage. Particularly when working with youth, the first two steps are crucial to gaining trust.

Step 1: Connecting before correcting (Romans 12:13; 1 Thessalonians 5:14)

> And we urge you, brothers and sisters, warn those who are idle and disruptive, encourage the disheartened, help the weak, be patient with everyone. (1 Thessalonians 5:14 NIV)

Try to imagine being Mariah as you prepare and pray before your first session. She is ashamed and embarrassed. She knows what she did is looked down on in the church. You want to be warm, caring but at the same time up front with her. Empathize but don't be overly saccharine; relate but don't act like you know how she feels. Depression can be confusing and hard to talk about for anyone, and maybe especially adolescents. Some don't know how to articulate their feelings; others are very guarded. When you add the trauma and embarrassment of a suicide attempt, you have a challenge to create a safe place for a teenager to share with you how she or he is thinking and feeling.

My opening line is typically something like this: "I know you don't want to be here. Your parents likely forced you to come, and you would rather be doing almost anything else."

This usually brings a slight smile or a head nod and breaks the ice (just a little!). I then tell them I am here for them and that what I share with parents is something we will agree on together. In Mariah's case it would also be important to say something like, "unless you are at significant risk of hurting yourself again, I may ask you to share things with your parents, but I will only give them a general status report with no details." That said, I would start by seeing both parents and Mariah together. I would ask all of them why they are there and what they hope to get from counseling. Parents often have much to say here and the teen often very little.

This is a good time to address the implicit conflict of interest that underlies most teen counseling. On the one hand, parents want to get their child help, on the other hand, teens often feel you are hired as their parents' agent and thus answer to them, share their agenda, and likely won't be someone they can confide in. So letting both parents and teens know what to expect in counseling is important. After you obtain the parents' perspective and clarify the goals and expectations related to confidentiality and care, it would be good to spend some time with Mariah without them.

Step 2: Assessing by drawing out the heart (Proverbs 18:13; 20:5)

> The purposes of a person's heart are deep waters,
>   but one who has insight draws them out. (Proverbs 20:5 NIV)

At the beginning of the counseling process, often all you will know is the presenting problem. In this case all you really know about Mariah is that she was depressed and attempted suicide. Early on you will want to assess her ongoing risk of self-harm because the risk increases once someone attempts suicide.[2]

Right now you want to hear her story. This might take two or three sessions to accomplish. While drawing out her heart is your goal early on, give hope through the Scriptures and a heart-targeting homework assignment in each session. One option would be to assign reading a psalm and answering questions as to how she relates to the author, the emotional context, and truth contained within. For instance, Psalm 130 points to God's mercy, connects to shame, and highlights God's comfort. This would help someone like Mariah see God has not rejected or left her and see the hope in God's purposes. Asking her to reflect on the character of God, how she can trust God in times of uncertainty, and the promise of his redeeming power will help her apply God's word to her situation.

When getting her story, be patient and ask questions like the following: What was it like growing up in your home? Who are your closest friends? How do you relate to your parents? What has been good, hard, or bad in your life? What do you like to do? What don't you like to do? Ask about music preferences, hobbies, and talents. Ask her to tell you about her relationship with God and her church experience. You want to know more about her than her problem of suicide risk or depression. As you unpack her story you will likely hear themes of loneliness, condemning self-talk, and the pain of feeling different, misunderstood, or unloved. Depression with teenagers can be masked by anger, withdrawal, or even a veneer of cheerfulness. Helping an adolescent to understand their emotions and express them honestly is part of preventing internalizing emotional pain. As you narrow in on what led to the attempt, you will want to assess factors that increased her depression, like loss, others she knows that struggle with self-harm tendencies, family conflict, drugs or alcohol use, stress, bullying, or abuse.

A simple way to categorize suicidal thinking is by determining whether your counselee is "not wanting to live" or is "wanting to die." In the first category you have low-risk counselees who feel depressed or somewhat hopeless and who may have occasional suicidal ideation. They typically have no plan and no real intent to hurt themselves, but any threat still should be taken seriously. Your plan would be preventative and purposeful, but with fewer restrictions or urgency. The second category "wanting to die" includes counselees who are at moderate to high risk of attempting suicide. They have a growing obsession with dying to escape pain, shame, or stress, with various levels of intent and premeditation. The development of a clear plan or access to easy means, along with increased isolation or mood changes means a counselee has moved into the high-risk category. Mariah went from low risk to high risk during a year or so. There were warning signs, but with teens it can be particularly hard to assess risk level. The most significant warning signs were her increased depression and growing isolation.

Step 3: Responding with truth and grace (Galatians 6:1–2; Ephesians 4:15)

> Brothers and sisters, if someone is caught in a sin, you who live by the Spirit should restore that person gently. But watch yourselves, or you also may be tempted. Carry each other's burdens, and in this way you will fulfill the law of Christ. (Galatians 6:1–2 NIV)

It is clear that Mariah struggles with depression, but is this the root of her problems or is it a fruit of something else (Luke 6:45)? As you trace heart themes in her life story it is likely that her struggle will be a mix of fear and despair. How does fear drive her hopelessness? Let's look back at her story to unlock patterns that will help you target the heart with Scriptures that might bring help and hope. Here are some stresses that emerged as I spoke with her:

- Demands of schoolwork
- Family conflict
- Fear of letting others down
- Never feeling good enough
- Friend cutting
- Social media comparisons and pressures
- Isolation and withdrawing from support
- Decreased interest in what used to provide pleasure
- Agitation and anger
- Loss of good friend
- Superficial church friends
- Medication side effects
- Overdose and hospitalization
- Shame and embarrassment
- Forced to come to church for help

These stresses and the patterns of thinking around them point to increasing fear and anxiety that has led to despairing thoughts. Your counsel and where you go in Scripture depend on her root issue. I have found that suicidal thinking is often rooted in a mix of anxiety and depression. While you may wonder if the medication is helping or hurting, this is not your focus nor your place to offer advice. If she or her parents ask about her medications, or if you or they are concerned about elevated suicidal thinking or other serious side effects, you should refer them back to their physician. Mariah did ask about her medications. We discussed side effects, and I recommended she (and her parents) not adjust or discontinue meds unless under a physician's care.

Once we have assessed both the risk level for self-harm and the root issues that led to the suicide attempt, we are ready to develop a care plan. Right now, Mariah feels like everyone is looking over her shoulder. A gentle approach with restoration in mind should guide your response. Trust is a two-way street. Mariah will need time to get to know and trust her care team. Team members will come to the home, sit in the counseling sessions, and help coach the family between sessions. They are all instructed to take an active interest in Mariah and let her know they are praying for her. This team is led by the counselor but should expand to a mentor/advocate for her, someone who can support the parents as friends and wise counsel, and others if you, Mariah, and her parents decide it would be helpful. This should be a long-term effort.

Remember that in crisis situations discretion is paramount; discreet communication will help avoid future deception and secrets. This family needs to be surrounded by a wise and caring community. The stigma of suicide is real and will need to be talked about in a way to help move from shame to a testimony of God's grace. While this is a stage where our main focus is on how to respond, we continue to assess Mariah by asking her questions and checking with her to verify that you have rightly identified her heart issues and that what you are saying fits or makes sense to her. Teens feel patronized or "talked at" too often. Including her by providing some options for homework is helpful and may decrease her resistance and increase her sense you respect her.

Give Mariah real and lasting hope. Take her to Scripture that will show her the compassion of our God who meets her in the midst of her pain. There she can find true soul rest. The Psalms is a place in Scripture for you to camp out with Mariah. Have her read Psalms that speak to suffering, shame, and God's protection and hope—Psalms 6, 23, 25, 32, 69, 73, and 139. I would ask her to write her own psalm after she understands the power of lament and talking honestly with God.

Here are some specific verses that could be used to help her in the midst of her current situation:

- "Come to me, all you who are weary and burdened, and I will give you rest. Take my yoke upon you and learn from me, for I am gentle and humble in heart, and you will find rest for your souls. For my yoke is easy and my burden is light." (Matthew 11:28–30 NIV)
- You who are my Comforter *in sorrow, my heart is faint within me.* (Jeremiah 8:18 NIV, emphasis added)
- My comfort *in my suffering is this: Your promise preserves my life.* (Psalm 119:50 NIV, emphasis added)

Sometimes teens think no one understands their pain. It can be powerful to show them Scriptures about suffering that acknowledge pain while remembering God's comfort and purposes.

> But we have this treasure in jars of clay to show that this all-surpassing power is from God and not from us. We are hard pressed on every side, but not crushed; perplexed, but not in despair; persecuted, but not abandoned; struck down, but not destroyed. (2 Corinthians 4:7–9 NIV)

Mariah's fear will need to be addressed in a few ways. Generalized anxiety points to a need to understand God's sovereignty, his care for her, and the power of prayer to connect her to God and his purposes, and her identity in Christ.

For the Spirit God gave us does not make us timid, but gives us power, love and self-discipline. (2 Timothy 1:7 NIV)

Do not be anxious about anything, but in every situation, by prayer and petition, with thanksgiving, present your requests to God. (Philippians 4:6 NIV)

Because of her fear of man and people pleasing she compares herself to others and feels she will never be good enough. This creates a never-ending cycle of performing and feeling like a failure.

Fear of man will prove to be a snare, but whoever trusts in the Lord is kept safe. (Proverbs 29:25 NIV)

Teens may question their faith. In Mariah's case her testimony was solid. She needs to know God has her—that he has not given up on her.

Being confident of this, that he who began a good work in you will carry it on to completion until the day of Christ Jesus. (Philippians 1:6 NIV)

Even though I walk through the darkest valley, I will fear no evil, for you are with me; your rod and your staff, they comfort me. (Psalm 23:4 NIV)

Therefore, my dear friends, as you have always obeyed—not only in my presence, but now much more in my absence—continue to work out your salvation with fear and trembling, for it is God who works in you to will and to act in order to fulfill his good purpose. (Philippians 2:12–13 NIV)

Most importantly, she needs to know not just what to do, but who she is in Christ. Spending time in the first three chapters of Ephesians can be a good way to help your counselees ground their identity in Christ.

Encourage Abiding in Christ and Community (John 15; Hebrews 3:12–14)

See to it, brothers and sisters, that none of you has a sinful, unbelieving heart that turns away from the living God. But encourage one another daily, as long as it is called "Today," so that none of you may be hardened by sin's deceitfulness. We have come to share in Christ, if indeed we hold our original conviction firmly to the very end. (Hebrews 3:12–14)

A large part of good biblical counsel is a combination of giving hope and getting counselees in the Word of God through heart-targeting homework. Teens are especially keen at discerning false hope or platitudes. Telling someone like Mariah "it will get better," or "it could have been worse" when they are depressed is a sure way to discourage them further.

Keep reading through the psalms with Mariah. The psalms resonate well with teens because they are raw, real, and even sometimes seem to border on irreverent. As they read, teens realize they can doubt, cry out, even get frustrated, but at the same time they can look to God. Teaching a teen to lament to God is a way to help them see just how much God cares.

Real hope is what she needs and is only found in Christ. Teaching her how to study the Bible, pray authentically, and fellowship deeply all point her to Christ and help her walk by faith. The goal for community and discipleship needs to be more than Bible knowledge. You can help Mariah learn how to pray through the Word and teach her to counsel herself using God's own words. The Spirit will use all of this to renew and transform Mariah (Romans 12:1–2).

A Word to Parents

Parents who have a teen who struggles with suicidal ideation or who has attempted suicide often don't know where to turn. Once their child is getting help they are relieved, but they still need to navigate through a maze of emotional and relational challenges. It can be a time where everyone walks in fear of another suicide attempt or of missing signs of depression. It is often a time of great introspection. *Where did we go wrong? How could we have missed this?* It can also be a time of desperation, shame, and feeling like a failure where it seems the church is the last place to go for help and healing.

Start by learning what you can about depression and the pressures of teens, but don't blame yourself. There are many reasons teens become anxious and depressed. You cannot protect them from all the variables that lead to depression and suicidal thinking. What you can do is take an interest in their lives. You can learn better ways to listen, relate, and care. At first, they may try to shut you out. Don't let this stop you from pressing in. I have found rejection is a big issue for parents.

Your teen may not want your influence at times, but they desperately need it. Let them know you are not going away.

Quality time often means quantity time. Your teen may need you to stop everything, take them for a drive (or somewhere with no distractions) and just listen. Understand that their life is more socially and emotionally complicated than yours may have been at their age. This is not the time to remind them how much time they waste on social media or how they need a better work ethic. Instead, ask them which friend understands them best and what they like most about that person. What are their struggles and biggest burdens? If you suspect self-harm or suicidal thinking may be happening, it is okay to talk about it. Remember, a question pricks the conscience, but an accusation can harden the heart. Be curious, but don't be so intrusive that they feel you are desperate. You can talk directly about cutting or suicide as an issue, but don't assume you know what they are thinking or doing.

Don't let your fear motivate you to overprotect. Ask questions, stay connected, but don't hover. Teen suicide prevention sites suggest that a candid conversation is not likely to lead to more temptation or self-destructive behavior and could prevent it.[3] If they do share and have thoughts about self-harm, respond carefully and don't react emotionally. Ask if there are things that they might use in a desperate moment. Get help involved based on severity, make the means harder to get to (lock up or remove pills or sharp objects, guns, or alcohol in the home). If you are unsure of their intentions and sense imminent risk or deception, always get them to acute care immediately.

Watch for things that can trigger self-harm. Depression or mood swings, changes in eating and sleeping habits, heightened anxiety, feelings of being trapped, withdrawal, agitation, being bullied, loss, family history of suicide or mental illness, drug or alcohol use, reckless behavior, and/or hopeless or suicidal talk. Mariah showed increasing signs of depression, isolation, stress, and the side effects of medications. These things together brought on a dark depression.

What may have helped to avoid the attempt? Perhaps parents admitting their need for marriage help. Maybe seeking godly counsel for her earlier, wise medical help, and a godly mentor she could confide in. But remember that depression and suicidal thoughts have many sources. If you notice anything you wish you had done differently, you can say, "I'm sorry" to God and your child. And, just as for your child, the challenge for you is to trust that God hears your prayers and is watching over your child. Ask your faithful Savior to build your house (Psalm 127). He will not fail you.

Mariah benefited from biblical counseling, and as her depression gradually lifted, she became a help to many other girls in her school. Her parents learned better ways to communicate with each other and her. This allowed them to build mutual trust and create parental support throughout her high school years. Mariah was blessed to have parents willing to learn, a church willing to come alongside her, and a counseling team that anchored their care in the gospel.

Churches and biblical counselors need to find ways to help teens with depression and anxiety before suicide attempts. We need to create better awareness of the issues and more options for help, including biblically based care groups and counseling options.

CHAPTER 10
HELPING CHILDREN WITH SHAME[1]

EDWARD T. WELCH

Steven, a smallish, eleven-year-old boy knows that every day at school will remind him he doesn't measure up. Reading and math are hard for him; attention is even harder. He already believes he is a "dummy," but the inevitable comments from other kids make everything harder. His problems fit the descriptions of Attention Deficit Disorder.

We all experience failure. We are able to do some things well and some things less well. But Steven was so experienced in failure that the unsuccessful events of life began to merge together into an identity. Failure was not something he did; it was who he was. Perhaps this was not voiced to him by a frustrated adult *every* day, but he heard it often enough to give consistent evidence that he was, indeed, a failure.

He is the oldest of three children. His sister is almost ten and doing fine both in school and with friends. His brother is seven, and Steven finds him to be a nuisance most of the time. His parents are concerned but have different ideas of how to help. His mother is gentle and non-confrontational. She would like to make life easier for him. His father is old-school: Best to face your problems, plow through them, stick with them until you have mastered them. He tends to be impatient, even though he had similar struggles in school. He doesn't understand his son and lives somewhere between frustration and giving up.

Homeschooling would seem to resolve his problems. There would be fewer daily comparisons. He could work at his own pace. But when something becomes your identity, a string of days without criticism is not enough to change it. It only moves it to the background, allowing it to become more apparent in other public settings. And homeschooling was not an option, given that both parents were working. So off he went to school.

His emotions usually ran one of two directions: "I am so dumb." Whether he said it under his breath—unconsciously—or said it with anger, it was his commentary on his life. Or he said, "You are so dumb." When emotions got the best of him, which they often did, he resorted to quotes from others about him that he, then, bequeathed to those around him. These words were one feature of his anger and less inhibited behavior. His self-control seemed to be getting worse as he got older.

On the positive side, he had a creative streak. He had an interest in how the house was arranged and decorated. His comments were interesting and sometimes carried out.

Where to Start?

Steven's parents are sending him to a counselor for two reasons: they want him fixed, and they want help. You are willing to see him as a way to come alongside the parents and help *them* be Steven's counselors. The first challenge is where to begin. You have a long list from which to choose. He is angry, and anger is always important and an easy way to get into Scripture, but you want to proceed carefully. Counselors want to say what is right, but that is easy. More difficult is to discern what is *most* important.

You notice that Steven is inattentive and seems to have academic weaknesses. Rather than focus on that, you suggest that the parents look into educational testing through their school as a way to gather more information about their son.

Failure is mingled throughout Steven's story. Since failure and shame are identified as critical matters of humanity, you decide to enter through that portal. The gist of the biblical story is that the Lord has a huge soft spot for those who are not accepted by others, who are different and don't quite measure up to some people's view of success. The reality is that shame is a dominant feature of our human experience, no matter our age, as well as a dominant theme in Scripture. Step one is to see it.

Words Describing Shame

Shame has a diverse vocabulary, and those different words can help us to see it more clearly. Here are a few:

Inferior	Weak
Inadequate	Rejected
Loser	Nothing
Different	Ignored
Failure	Poor
Misfit	Unattractive
Stupid	Unpopular
Embarrassed	Wanting to hide
Stared at	Last
Unwanted	Bullied

These feelings can be painful, dominating, and fluctuating in intensity. As parents and counselors, we recognize that these struggles don't simply disappear over time, though maturity might push them into the background for some children at some times. Where do go next?

"Pour Out Your Heart" (Psalm 62:8)

With children and teens, a clear agenda is no guarantee that you will get there. Children might have no interest in speaking to you about what is important, and they might not even be able to identify what is important. Children need skill to put their emotions into speech. So a counselor can quickly feel that the counseling relationship is in jeopardy before it begins, and it might be. But you know that in God's household, we try to put our troubles into words and speak those words to the Lord. This means you hope to draw out the child—the more he speaks, the better.

"Steven, God likes you to talk to him. He likes you to tell him what was great about your day, what was hard about your day, and where you need help. I am going to talk to him about those things. Do you want to pray too?"

The psalms are examples of how we can speak to our Father. They also teach us how to talk with each other. The psalms often move naturally from talking to the Lord, talking *about* the Lord with each other, praising the Lord together, and crying out to the Lord together. We invite a child to speak with us because that's what we do with God *and* with each other.

If the child or teen is reluctant, they can still learn this lesson from parents, teachers, Sunday school teachers, and others, so an unproductive time with a child is not the end of fruitful involvement. But you hope to engage them personally as much as possible. To this end, you could put words on Steven's experience. An example follows:

"Steven, you don't seem to like school at all. Can you imagine anything that is as bad as school?"

"No, school is the worst."

"Sometimes, when the teacher talks, you don't know what she is saying. People always tell you to try harder. You can feel different from everyone else, and, usually, we don't want to feel different.

"I just don't like it."

Progress is difficult at this point. If a parent is present, you could ask the parent to help Steven find words that describe his experience.

Meet the Tax Collector

Counseling moves back and forth between knowing the child and knowing God's words to the person. As you consider Scripture, shame can be found in words such as *dishonor, poor, weak, oppressed*, and, of course, *shame*. Key people include barren women, lepers, tax collectors, and Samaritans. The challenge is to have at least one meaningful connection between the child and Scripture.

Tax collectors were among the outcasts. No one liked them; no one wanted to be associated with them. But Jesus is different than the rest of us. Jesus likes outcasts because they need his help, and it turns out that he was an outcast too. He invited tax collectors to eat with him, which was another way of saying, "Please join me, you are fully accepted here" (Matthew 9:11). One of the better-known stories of the New Testament is about a tax collector who wanted to see Jesus but assumed he was too bad to get close. But Jesus, even with a large crowd all around him, saw Zacchaeus up in a tree, knew his name, and spent the afternoon at his house. So Zacchaeus became Jesus's friend. After that, Zacchaeus treated people differently because Jesus had treated him so kindly (Luke 19:1–8).

The tax collector went from outcast to someone Jesus knows by name. From outcast to someone Jesus honors with a home visit. From outcast to someone who becomes a friend of Jesus. No wonder Zacchaeus changed so dramatically. How could he *not* take on the character of the one who honored him so?

This story might draw a child in to Scripture. If not, keep looking for ways to know the child, put words on his experience, pray together, and surprise him with how Jesus accepts him with understanding and kindness.

Put on New Clothes

Another teaching about shame is that Jesus gives us new clothes. Most children have some sense that the right clothes—the cool clothes—can bring some dignity to life, and the wrong clothes can embarrass. Throughout biblical history, clothes were connected to status. This story appears almost immediately in Scripture when humanity was identified as naked and unashamed, only to soon be naked and needing clothes.

The beginning of the conversation might go like this: "Most of us have clothes we really like to wear, and we have other clothes we wish we never had to wear. Do you see these flip-flops? For some reason, I really like them. I think they are cool. Do you have any favorite thing to wear?"

"I like clothes that have the same color. And my black sneakers are my favorite."

One way into Scripture is through Zechariah's vision of a priest named Joshua who found himself in the heavenly courts in ratty, dirty clothes (Zechariah 3:1–5). Satan was quick to accuse and have the priest expelled. His argument was that the priest was unfit to be in God's presence and should be made an outcast. The Lord, however, rebuked Satan and then dressed the priest—who represents us all before the Lord—in pure vestments and a clean turban. The style of dress might not be a modern one, but the outfit was beautiful. The turban added the royal touch of a crown. The point of the story is that Jesus takes away our guilt and shame, and he makes us presentable.

Where can we find adequate covering? This question is found throughout Scripture. It ends with wedding garments that cover all of God's people (Revelation 19:7–8). In the meantime, think Joseph's coat, the priests' garments (Exodus 28:2), even the clothes God gives us for spiritual warfare (Ephesians 6:10–15). Since Scripture has different images of those clothes, counselors can take some liberty in imagining them.

"When Jesus brings you into his house, he gives you new clothes that are the best. He actually makes you look strong—like a soldier with spears and swords and armor and shields. You can see this if you look closely." (Then read Ephesians 6:10–17.)

Do Some Boasting

When we sink under the weight of rejection, we often try to attach ourselves to someone of reputation. For adults it can be a sports team; for teens it can be a celebrity or a favorite band; for younger children it might be a popular friend. In other words, we recognize that our achievements will never be enough to pick us up and make us part of a group. We need the reputation of another. And that is the essence of the gospel of Jesus.

> Thus says the LORD: "Let not the wise man boast in his wisdom, let not the mighty man boast in his might, let not the rich man boast in his riches, but let him who boasts boast in this, that he understands and knows me, that I am the LORD who practices steadfast love, justice, and righteousness in the earth. For in these things I delight, declares the LORD." (Jeremiah 9:23–24)

When we are with Jesus we have the greatest friend imaginable. He has called us his own. He has brought us into his inner circle and shared his intimate thoughts and plans. His words to us, "I am with you," are *the* way to respond to our feelings of rejection and failure.

A Word to Parents

You have the perfect foundation: you love your child, you want to grow in Christ as you parent him, and we believe that the Lord hears us in our time of need. Our question now is, how can you love your child even more wisely and in a way that the two of you are united?

Love begins with patience and kindness. The impatience of anger is never helpful, and, for a boy who is already laid low by his failures and the comments of others, anger will tear him down even more.

Love wants a growing knowledge of the other person. You will want to know your child in a way that enables you to speak words that describe his experience. Others, like teachers, physicians, Sunday school teachers, and family members, can contribute to an even fuller profile. Whatever strategies come from this knowledge will include small goals and small steps for growth. For example, if your child is weak with numbers, you can revise your expectations, work with him more patiently, and work at shorter bursts that might gradually be extended.

Love looks for and enjoys the strengths of others. There are benefits to persevering in challenging matters, but parents can accentuate the strengths of their children more than weaknesses. And, once we begin to look for a person's strengths, we can usually find many.

Through all this, you will want humility. You will do best when you see yourselves as needy before Christ. Then you will pray for your child, pray for yourselves, ask others to pray, and be quick to seek advice.

You will also do best when you see your child's struggles as *more* similar to your own, rather than less. Reputation, failure, rejection, and shame—these belong to us all. Imagine Steven's father seeing his own quest for achievement and a competing reality shown in the gospel in which he trusts in Jesus and his achievements. Imagine being able to confess how you would like to boast about something in yourselves, and how you want to grow to boast more of Jesus.

Our failure, rejection and shame can help us appreciate Jesus's death and resurrection. He was rejected by Jews and Gentiles. He was even rejected by his friends. The events leading up to his crucifixion accumulated one degrading act upon another. Jesus was insulted, spit upon, whipped, and treated as though he were nothing. On the cross he was naked as he cried out "My God, why have you forsaken me" (Matthew 27:46). In all this, he both shared in and carried our guilt and shame.

Gradually, the message comes through. God's people are the ones familiar with failure, rejection, and shame. Those who rest in their achievements do not need him. Instead, the evidence that we are his people is having learned that achievements are an unstable foundation for life and that we need Jesus. Who would have thought that a child's failure and rejection would take both the child and his parents into the heart of God and the good news of his death and resurrection?

> God chose the foolish things of the world to shame the wise; God chose the weak things of the world to shame the strong. He chose the lowly things of this world and the despised things—and the things that are not—to nullify the things that are, so that no one may boast before him. It is because of him that you are in Christ Jesus, who has become for us wisdom from God—that is, our righteousness, holiness and redemption. Therefore, as it is written: "Let the one who boasts boast in the Lord." (1 Corinthians 1:27–31 NIV)

Children and Their Bodies

CHAPTER 11
TALKING WITH CHILDREN ABOUT SEX
KEVIN CARSON

Ben's Story

Ben was a thirteen-year-old boy who had undergone tremendous changes in the previous two years. Physically, he had grown about six inches, and he had an increasingly deeper voice. But this was not the biggest change that had occurred in his life. A year earlier Ben's dad Kyle had walked away from his family and discontinued playing a role in Ben's day-to-day life. As his pastor for many years, I carefully observed Ben's response throughout the divorce. He appeared to remain open to conversation, sensitive to his mother, and committed to honoring God in his response.

Recently while putting away laundry in Ben's room, Shelly noticed Ben lying in his bed watching a video on her iPad. It struck her as strange that he was under the covers in the middle of the day and that he seemed very uncomfortable with her in the room. A feeling of unease grew when she left the room to grab some additional laundry and reentered to see him continuing to lie there.

Shelly quietly put the laundry away, sat on the side of Ben's bed, and prepared herself for an awkward conversation.

"Ben, it's unusual for you to be in bed in the middle of the day. You feeling okay?"

"Yes, Mom," Ben mumbled, turning his face away from her. Shelly continued, "What are you watching?"

Ben embarrassingly fought for words. He sheepishly admitted, "Well, I'm looking at some pictures of girls."

Alarm bells and a flood of questions rushed through her head as she sought to find the right way to respond. She took a deep breath.

"Girls? What are the girls doing? What are you talking about?"

"Just girls, Mom," Ben quietly responded.

Shelly became quite suspicious that in addition to whatever he was looking at online, he was also masturbating. The thought sent chills up and down her spine as she found it harder to breathe normally. This was a day she had dreaded. After a few seconds that felt like minutes, Shelly fumbled through her next words.

"What are you doing under the covers? Why don't you sit up here beside me so we can talk?"

"I'd rather not, Mom," Ben said, his face increasingly red and his eyes beginning to tear up.

His sensitivity did not surprise Shelly. Of her three children, Ben had always seemed the tenderest. As he was growing up, whenever he faced discipline or the thought of it, his reaction typically included shyness, tears, and blushed face.

She pressed further. "Ben, what were you watching?"

"Videos, Mom," Ben said.

"Videos?" Shelly repeated in a somewhat tense voice. "What exactly about girls were you watching?"

The momentary silence weighed heavy until he responded softly. "Mom, I'd rather not show you. It was just girls."

She waited until Ben slowly showed her a glance at the screen. It was a naked girl.

"Ben, when did you start looking at this? Where did you find this?"

"When I was at Zack's house," Ben replied.

"At Zach's house? When? What were you doing? Where were his parents?"

At this point, Ben's tears began to flow down his face. Shelly reached over, hugged him, and encouraged him to tell her the story.

Ben explained that he and Zach were on Zach's phone watching some behind-the-scenes clips of Star Wars on You-Tube when a picture of a pretty girl appeared on a gaming commercial in the middle of the clip. Zack had clicked on it.

The link took them to a video game commercial with other picture-associated advertisements on the page. Most of the advertisement links were animated, but one of them was of a real girl. In mere moments and a few curious clicks, the boys unintentionally stumbled into a pornographic website. Both Zach and Ben were shocked, but they hadn't exited the website.

Shelly asked, "Ben, why did you keep watching it? That is porn." She told him they could talk more about it soon and asked him to give her the iPad.

Shelly's heart broke for her son. The realization began to set in that her son's innocence was robbed by an ad on You-Tube at a friend's house. She simultaneously grew angry at the producer of the pornography, Zach's parents for not filtering his phone internet, and herself.

Shelly had planned to talk with her boys when she thought each individual boy was ready. However, with Ben having two younger brothers, Shelly thought he was developmentally behind many of the children his same age. Plus, she thought her house was "locked down" so that he could not see anything questionable. She had feared he might see something inappropriate somewhere, but had hoped Ben would just turn away quickly if it actually happened. Shelly also knew that with all the recent difficulties in their home, she had conveniently put off the conversation.

Speaking with a mix of desperation, passion, anger, and concern, Shelly asked for my help. "What am I supposed to do? How am I supposed to deal with him? Will you please take a few minutes as a godly man in his life to talk with him?"

Biblical Principles to Guide Conversations with Children about Sex

Ben provides us a great case study to consider as counselors who help children and their parents maneuver through these unfamiliar waters—conversations that relate both to sex in general and masturbation and pornography in particular. The most ideal scenario in this type of counseling situation would be to equip parents to have these conversations with their own children, as parents should be the primary figures in a child's life to set the foundation for understanding God's design for sex. There are many situations such as Ben's, however, where a parent is either absent from the picture or not in a strong relationship with their child, and you as the counselor may be called upon to stand in the gap for this child and help them navigate these significant issues.

Each conversation you have with a child or teen will be different, as each young person will vary in temperament, prior knowledge, and relationship with the Lord. Keep in mind that in all scenarios, a biblical discussion about sex, set in the context of a robust understanding of God and his design, will likely take place over a series of conversations, not just one.

We can see how Ben's eyes were opened to a Pandora's box of new ideas, thoughts, and emotions related to sex. The challenge becomes how to shepherd his heart toward future sexual pleasures found within the context of God's plan and God's timing, and how to help him gain a vision for God's glory with his thoughts and actions. This is particularly difficult to do when the world around him offers promises of pleasure and excitement now.

Yes, Ben has made choices that fail to honor God by watching pornography, indulging in masturbation, and allowing his heart to be carried away by lust. However, as counselors we must understand that Ben is also a sufferer. He is a young boy struggling through not only the pressures of early adolescence, but also the intense grief of his father's abandonment. This must be taken into account as we seek to encourage in him a heart that honors the Lord. As he grapples with these things, the culture provides easy-access content, his body surges toward full sexual maturity, and the physical, visual, and mental stimulation brings great pleasure to his aching heart.

The first time Ben and I met, I asked him tell me his story. He explained how he had not really paid attention to girls before he and his friend stumbled upon pornography. However, since he had subsequently continued watching pornographic videos regularly and talking with his friend about what they watched, he often struggled with sexual fantasy and masturbation. I used my worksheet titled "The Big Picture" to help Ben begin to put this struggle in context spiritually, emotionally, and physically. This worksheet helps set the stage for interpreting circumstances and opportunities in light of five foundational questions concerning life's purpose.

THE BIG PICTURE

Who is God?

How do I live the way God desires?

What is my purpose in life?

Who am I?

What are my responsibilities?

When thinking about where you want to begin to engage Ben, you may be tempted to focus first on the presenting problem and talk to Ben immediately about pornography and masturbation. Ben really needs to know first the larger context surrounding any conversation about sin, suffering, and struggle. Ben needs to understand who he is, who God is, and why God made him. Without this foundation, the counsel that you give in addressing sex and pornography will probably not be as effective as you hope.

What is my purpose in life?

After hearing Ben's story, I began by guiding him in a discussion about the purpose of his life. Perhaps Ben had never stopped to think deeply about this. I talked with Ben about all the pleasures and good gifts God provides for us each day.

"Ben, you talked about how the people on the videos seemed to be having so much fun, and you referenced how it feels good to masturbate and think about sex. I think you have hit on something important to consider. Let's make a list together of all the things in life that you find pleasurable." Ben and I had fun as we made a lengthy list of some of our favorite things, including eating ice cream, tossing a football, and watching movies with friends.

I asked Ben, "Do you know where all these good gifts come from?" Ben easily identified God as the giver of these favorite pastimes. We laughed together as we talked about God being the absolute *best God ever*, which allowed me to discuss God's best gifts of Christ, salvation, sanctification, and service to others. This is where I introduced 2 Corinthians 5:14–15 alongside verse 9, where Paul says he makes it his aim to live a Christ-centered, Christ-honoring life.

The best motivation for Ben to learn to live for Jesus first is the love that Christ has for him. Paul wrote, "For the love of Christ compels us, because we judge thus: that if One died for all, then all died; and He died for all, that those who live should live no longer for themselves, but for Him who died for them and rose again" (2 Corinthians 5:14–15 NKJV).

Like each of us, Ben has been put on this earth to glorify God. It is the transforming love of Jesus that will ultimately motivate Ben to pursue a lifestyle that seeks to honor and magnify the Lord. An understanding of the grace that God offers him through Jesus will enable him to see his life as one of thanksgiving, not living under a list of rules but living as a rescued, beloved child. Essentially, I want to help Ben begin to understand that God is so good, loving, and generous that it is a joy to desire becoming more like Christ and honoring him with every part of our lives.

Who is God?

During my second meeting with Ben, we focused on the next two portions of "The Big Picture" worksheet. We started with the second question, "Who is God?"

Ben and I had already identified God as the giver of good gifts. The next step forward was to consider God as Creator, Lord, and Savior. Genesis 1–3 helped form the basis of our conversation.

Creator. I explained to Ben that as our Creator, God intricately designed us and knows more than anyone else what is best for us.

Lord. Because God is God, he gets to set the standard for what is right, wrong, good, bad, wise, unwise, appropriate and inappropriate. He rules the universe. At the end of the day, God is the one whose opinion matters most.

Savior. Ben and I looked together at Genesis 3 to explore the necessity of God as Savior. Ben recalled the story of Adam and Eve in the garden of Eden. We discussed the fall of Adam and all mankind after him. I emphasized the fact that Adam and Eve (and all of us) could not save themselves from the just punishment of sin; however, God came looking for them in love and grace. God moved toward them to redeem them, and God has done this for Ben through sending Jesus to die on the cross.

After this dialogue, I asked Ben to help me answer the question, "Who is God?" He explained that God is the Creator, Lord, and Savior. This foundational understanding would help set the parameters for how we would eventually discuss sex. God is the Creator, Lord, and Savior over sex too. The world's voice and values are not the authority on this matter—God is.

Who am I?

We moved on to the third question on "The Big Picture" worksheet. "Who am I?" helps Ben see who he is in light of who God is. Ben is a created being, is made in the image of God, is dearly loved, and is in Christ.

Created. I said to Ben, "This may seem like a silly question, but if God is the Creator and he created you, doesn't that make you part of his creation?" Ben agreed. I went on to explain to him how although that is true, many times we act as if we are the creator and think we have the final say in our lives. Our sinful nature wants us to be our own ultimate authority, but this does not change reality. The truth is that we are called to submission to him.

Image-bearer. I went on to explain that when God created us, he created us in his image (Genesis 1:26–28; Isaiah 43:7). This was crucial for shaping how Ben saw himself and others. I used the example of a copy machine. I emphasized the idea that a copy is an image or in the likeness of the original. I continued, "Ben, you are made in the image of or the likeness of God. God made you to both be like him and function like him. As an image of God, you are a special person with personal value."

As Ben listened, I asked, "If you are valuable because you are made in the image of God, what do you think is also true

166

about other people around you? What is their value?" Ben told me that they are valuable as well because they were also made in the image of God. I agreed, and we discussed how because of this truth, it matters how we treat others. We must treasure, respect, and support the image of God in others. Therefore, any behavior that minimizes the significance of the image of God in another individual person is sinful.

I then made my first reference to pornography and explained how it was a violation of this principle. We talked about the fact that pornography disregards and disrespects the image of God in others and makes them an object of our lust rather than treating them with the respect, dignity, and love they deserve.

Loved and in Christ. We circled back around to God's love because I wanted to continue to emphasize this as the motivation for all of our obedience. I encouraged him, "Ben, remember how deeply you are loved? God demonstrated his ultimate act of love for you by sending Jesus to the cross in your place. As a child of God, you have been made new and given his Spirit to help you live out of this identity" (Ephesians 4:1; James 1:13–18; 2 Peter 1:3–11).

I explained this further to Ben. "Remember how God gives the best gifts? One of his gifts to us is the incredible pleasure of sex, but it's a gift that's only meant to be opened in his time and according to his plan. He does this because in his loving-kindness, he wants you to enjoy this gift in the right way and in the right time in order to protect and bless you and your future wife. As you think about sex, I want you to think about how God loves you, is for you, and that he's inviting you to come under his lordship and trust that his ways are best."

What are my responsibilities?

The first three questions on "The Big Picture" worksheet set a solid foundation for the rest of my appointments with Ben. The following two questions provide guidance for his day-to-day living.

Ben and I began to look at some of the practical steps that he could take to set himself up for success regarding his struggle with pornography and masturbation. We spoke with his mother to reestablish the internet safeguards, set up accountability at home (e.g., use of the computer by permission only in public spaces for specific purposes), and began meditating on some important Scripture passages from our first meeting. The simple worksheet allowed Ben to see a structure for our time together.

Love the Lord your God and your neighbor. Ben and I discussed how the first and second great commandments provide the best guidance for how to live for God's glory (Matthew 22:37–40). Since God has been so gracious to us, what greater joy is there than to love him and our neighbor in return? The heart of sin clamors for us to love self, but by contrast our new life in Christ calls us to love God supremely and others (our neighbor) sincerely. Jesus summarizes everything in the Bible by the simple statement, "Love the Lord your God with all your heart, soul, and mind." This is what God wants most of all.

Further, to love your neighbor means that you desire what is best for others and you sacrificially serve them out of love for God. At this point, I made connections for Ben related to sex and sexual lust. Loving God supremely and your neighbor sincerely means that your love for God will motivate you to seek to honor him and others above yourself. I used a series of questions to help him think through what this might look like in relation to his sexual desires. Does looking at pornography demonstrate loving God supremely and our neighbor sincerely? Does a practice of masturbation fit within the two great commandments? If we are to love God and neighbor most, what place does that leave for your love and desire for sexual pleasure?

Have sex for the glory of God. I explained to Ben, "God's design for sex includes lots of pleasure and is a way for you to serve your future spouse in God's timing. The problem you have is not a problem with sex. The struggle is wanting to enjoy the pleasures of sex in *your* timing and not in *God's* timing. You need to instead value and look forward to the time reserved exclusively for you and your future wife to enjoy the pleasures and joys of sex according to God's plan." We talked about how God graciously provides the gift of sex not just to have children, but as a pleasurable way to serve one's spouse and to communicate love and commitment to each other for the glory of God (Proverbs 5:18–19; 1 Corinthians 6:19–7:5).

How do I live the way God desires?

The final question on this worksheet provides Ben with a way forward. Why leave this question until last? A child needs to understand and comprehend the big picture before getting a list of do's and don'ts. Now that he understands better the two things for which he is responsible (regarding biblical sexuality), we focus on his daily decisions.

Walk in the Spirit. Galatians 5:16–26 provides help for Ben's daily living. I explained to him, "Ben, you are in a battle. You may not have known that, but the desire to give in to lust fights against the desire to love God supremely, love others, and practice self-control."

We looked at this passage together and talked through ways Ben could be encouraged to walk in the Spirit—that is, recognize the Spirit's presence and power as he goes through his day. We discussed how Bible reading, prayer, accountability with Christian friends, journaling, and reviewing his identity in Christ daily will greatly strengthen his walk with Christ and encourage the fruit of love, faithfulness, and self-control to grow in his life. I also reminded him of the importance and blessing of making every effort to honor the Lord (2 Peter 1:3–11).

Wait in anticipation as an act of love toward Christ and others. Using 1 Thessalonians 4:1–8 as our backdrop, we discussed living for God's glory related to sex in daily living. It all comes back to the first question on this worksheet about purpose of life. The apostle Paul stresses how followers of Christ must live and please God. He emphasizes that this is God's will—to have self-control regarding sexual lusts and behavior. This demonstrates love and respect to one's neighbors as well.

"Ben, as one who is called to be holy, you must live pure in regard to all your sexual desires, impulses, and actions. In fact, when you do not, you do not simply disappoint your mom and your pastor as your human authority, you reject God's authority. God gave you a changing body which naturally desires sexual pleasures. But how you respond to those changes, what you wish for, how you view girls, and how you treat them greatly matters. God cares and loves you just as he cares and loves all the girls in your life as well."

We reviewed the importance of his own personal wisdom choices to put him in a strong position to say no to his flesh and yes to the Spirit. I asked him to begin a list of key choices going forward regarding internet use, watching YouTube with friends, conversations with other guys, and what to do when tempted to masturbate. We planned to review the list during our next session and discuss the way a relationship looks according to God's plan.

A Word to Parents

Children need honest and beneficial conversations with their parents about sexuality. Like Shelly, many parents tend to stumble along through these conversations, feeling awkward and ill-equipped. The reality is, however, that combined with easy access to pornography, the culture's changing views on marriage and sex, and the trend toward decreasing family time, it's never been more important for Christian parents to be the first and best source of information about God's good design for sex.

Oftentimes when parents first discover evidence of a child's struggle with issues related to sex, sexual expression, or pornography, they tend to panic. Take hope, dear parent, because God provides you grace and strength as you seek to parent for his glory, and he uses your imperfect efforts for the good of your children. With God's grace, parents can demonstrate to their child that this is not a taboo topic and that they are a safe place to come for counsel.

Start the conversation early

Like Shelly, many parents wait too long to begin talking with children about sex. When a parent waits until after the child engages in problematic behavior to discuss these key issues, the parent fails to proactively train, shepherd, and disciple the child (Proverbs 22:6; Ephesians 6:4). So start early. Begin to discuss biblical sexuality as situations arise in life, for instance when your young child asks innocent questions at bath time, when he or she grimaces as Mom and Dad kiss, or when he or she sees sexual references pop up in media. A simple conversation should begin by kindergarten age.

In initial conversations, the parent should explain basic anatomy and the general role of the reproductive system. It is important to use proper terminology so that a child understands the real names of body parts and knows there is nothing shameful about the body. By early elementary, emphasize that God's design is good and that he has planned for a special way for a husband and wife to express love to each other and enjoy pleasure together. As the child ages, include more of the details discussed above with Ben.

Children will appreciate and respond positively to honesty and candor. If your child asks questions, then answer honestly. The locker room, social media, and Google searches should not teach your children. The parent bears the responsibility of teaching, training, and discipling (Deuteronomy 6:6–9). As you teach, seek to speak in age-appropriate ways with clarity and without euphemistic confusion.

Set up safeguards

As parents who seek to serve their children well, set up your home and electronics to limit your child's access to inappropriate images. As in this story, it is impossible to shield your child from everything. However, internet filters, accountability software, and clear household rules will set the standard for responsible media use.

As you raise your child, the primary goal is *not* to keep him or her totally sheltered from the world. However, doing everything you can to shield them from inappropriate content will help train your child in godliness as you shepherd them toward a deep love for the Lord.

Specifically related to phones, help the child understand that a smartphone has specific uses that are helpful for daily living. Making a phone call, taking a picture, looking up directions, and managing calendars can all be done conveniently from a phone. Parents should particularly be on guard against modeling unwise phone habits, like endless social media scrolling, addictive game playing, and other time-wasting activities. This can undermine the messages you are trying to teach your children.

Watch your reaction

One of the key goals of conversation with your children is having *another* conversation. A parent's measured response to a child's questions or to a troubling scenario opens the door to further engagement, investigation, discovery, involvement, instruction, and hope. Paying attention to key skills in this conversation typically yields better and more fruitful conversations.

- *Make sure you stay calm.* When Shelly observed Ben's suspicious behavior, she chose to remain calm and act as normal as possible. As Shelly heard about the friend's house and YouTube, she calmly asked more questions, keeping her tone as measured as possible.
- *Do your best to listen well.* Listen for facts. Make sure you do not assume your child's motives or assume

your child is lying. As you ask questions, divide your time between fruit issues (what was said, felt, and done) and root issues (what is believed, desired, longed for, and loved). As you listen to your child's answer, ask yourself, *What part of the story is missing? What vocabulary do I not understand?*

- *Seek to interpret what you hear.* As you hear your child's answers to your questions, seek to discern the heart of your child. Is your child's heart rebellious, curious, or suffering (1 Thessalonians 5:14)? In Ben's case he accidentally viewed pornography, which sets him up to potentially suffer for some time as he struggles to connect what he saw with his own physical development and what honors God.

- *Offer your child an open door for further conversations, questions, and observations.* All people function best, talk more, and speak more honestly in a safe environment. If your child believes that answering your questions, asking his or her own questions, or confessing particular sins will be met with exaggerated tones, quick responses, assumed motives, sarcasm, or ridicule, the opportunity for meaningful conversations will be minimal.

Balance holiness, discipline, mercy, and grace

The confluence of various physiological, mental, spiritual, relational, and cultural pressures provide many opportunities for children and teens to struggle between a desire to honor God and a desire to fit in with the culture and pursue sensual desires.

Do not be surprised that your child sins. Sins of masturbation, pornography, same-sex exploration, and heterosexual sex are common areas of temptation as puberty sets in. If your child begins to sin in one of these areas, remember that all sexual sins flow out of a discontent heart longing for self-pleasure rather than prioritizing love of God and others (James 1:13–18).

Understand that your child, like you, both suffers and sins. As you engage your children, therefore, do so with understanding and grace. Hold out before them the importance and joy of honoring the Lord even in suffering. Where they struggle with sin, help them as necessary. Certain privileges may need to be limited and other safeguards practiced to help promote a better and safer environment more productive for growth and godliness. Along the journey, recognize that your child needs the same mercy and grace you so desperately need.

As you prepare your own heart for these interactions, pray earnestly for God to work in your child's heart, for God to help you see your own heart as well, and for God to provide all of you the awareness of his grace along the journey. See individual incidences and interactions as part of a larger conversation. Although at times you may not see the progress, trust God that he will use your conversations in beneficial ways in your child's life. As much as you love your child and desire what is best, God infinitely loves him or her and he works alongside you as you strive to be a faithful parent.

CHAPTER 12
TALKING ABOUT SEXUAL IDENTITY
TIM GEIGER, HARVEST USA

Alex

Now fifteen, Alex is the fourth of five children. He feels like
he has never fit in—either in his family or as a male. Alex is
the youngest of four boys and also has a younger sister. Each
of Alex's brothers seems to be the epitome of masculinity:
big, burly, athletic, confident, and popular with both gals
and guys. Alex feels like his parents are not too interested in
him—they seem more engaged with his brothers and sister.

Alex never felt included by his brothers in their play or in
their friendships. Because he was four years younger than his
next older brother, he felt like the perpetual "baby" among the
older boys. When Alex's sister was born just two years after
him, he noticed how everyone fawned over and celebrated her.

As Alex noticed the difference in attention between his sister and himself, around the age of four his behavior began to
change—he assumed female roles in play, started acting more
typically feminine, and preferred culturally feminine toys and
colors. His parents tried to discourage Alex's culturally di-
vergent preferences, and sometimes Alex would retreat to his
room—or even just into his mind—for sanctuary. But the attention, even though it was negative, was still attention. As he
grew older, Alex began to view himself as a female and began
secretly trying on some of his mother's clothing and makeup.

176

When he started high school last year, Alex found a new group of friends who seemed more accepting of him than his parents and siblings. He came out to them last year as transgender, and a few weeks later he took the risk of publicly wearing lipstick at school. Since that time, Alex has progressively taken bigger risks—adding rouge, mascara, and a ribbon to tie his shoulder-length hair into a ponytail. He's asked his friends to call him "Alexis."

Up to this point he's only expressed himself as female at school, not at home. Alex hasn't decided when, but he is certain that he wants to come out to his family and tell them he's trans and that he wants to transition to a female. He's waiting for the right timing to tell his family, but he's scared to death of what they'll say.

Devin

Devin is an intelligent, creative, and insightful twelve-year-old girl with a hard story. She has a history of relational and emotional abandonment. Her heart has been wounded many times over her young life. And she's a lesbian.

Devin's father never wanted to be part of her life, and Devin's mother was addicted to opioids when she gave birth. Devin's mother's addiction and chaotic lifestyle meant that she was often physically and emotionally unavailable for her daughter. Then, when Devin was six, her mother died of an overdose.

After her mother's death, Devin was placed with her mother's parents. Though they loved her, they struggled to demonstrate that love—and frequently failed. Devin's grandparents had resented their daughter's poor choices and cut her off from the family years earlier. They were shocked to learn of Devin's existence after their daughter's death. Moreover, they were not expecting to change their empty-nest lifestyle in order to accommodate a granddaughter.

Having failed to bond with her mother, Devin then struggled to bond with her grandparents. As a socially awkward girl, she also struggled to connect with peers at school and at church.

Years of counseling haven't helped Devin much. Although she gained some insight into herself and learned some social skills, she always felt different—shut off somehow—from others, particularly from other girls her own age. She now had a few friends, but she felt, well, *different*.

A few months ago at a sleepover at a friend's house, she met a girl new to the school. Chloe took a particular interest in Devin and spent nearly the entire evening talking with her. She also talked Devin up to the other girls. When the lights finally went out, Chloe made certain that her sleeping bag was next to Devin's. Chloe proceeded to kiss Devin goodnight—but on the lips. For an hour, the two girls were physically engaged with one another. Chloe's self-confidence and interest in Devin felt intoxicating. Devin felt *different* with her. And it was a good kind of *different*.

The affirmation felt like new life to Devin. The next day they met up again. Soon they were openly girlfriends. Finally, Devin had someone who loved her and made her feel special. Chloe filled in all of the love deficits that had existed for her entire life.

Living in a Broken World

Both Alex and Devin have lived feeling isolated and alone for most of their days on earth. Alex has felt like an outsider in his family, and Devin likewise has suffered from feeling unloved, unwanted and abandoned. Outcasts. A ray of hope came into their lives when they received acceptance from others.

As a biblical counselor, you know that the acceptance, good feelings, and satisfaction these relationships are currently yielding won't last into eternity because they don't function according to God's design for relationships. You also know that life becomes harder when we try to function in a way that God did not design us to function.

That's a part of what Alex and Devin are each facing. Each of them is misusing something good given to them by God (namely, sex and gender). Let's stop for a moment and briefly consider God's design for sex and gender. These topics are developed significantly in Scripture, and, given the scope and length of this chapter, we can barely scrape their surfaces here.[1]

Knowing God's design

Sex. God tells us in his Word that sex is a gift reserved only for married spouses,[2] in order that they would become one body (Genesis 2:24; 1 Corinthians 6:16). This gift is also meant to be oriented toward the pleasure and edification of the spouse, not primarily oriented toward one's own pleasure (see 1 Corinthians 7:3–5).[3] While spouses are invited to create an environment where their mates might experience joy and intimacy, the experience of sex is meant to be pleasurable for both (see Song of Solomon 4:1–8:7). Sex is also meant to regularly proclaim that the safety and beauty of the marriage covenant declared by the two spouses is still in force and that the bonds of love that hold the spouses together remains strong.

Gender. Scripture doesn't explicitly tell us as much about gender as it does sex and sexuality, but there is much we can infer from what is said directly and how gender is spoken of throughout the whole of Scripture. What we can readily glean is that God established only two binary genders (male and female) in creation (Genesis 1:27). Additionally, God sovereignly from eternity past assigned one gender or another to each of his particular image-bearers (Psalm 139:13–16; Jeremiah 1:5). One's God-assigned gender is unchangeable and eternal (Deuteronomy 22:5).[4]

Lastly, although not from Scripture, we should remember that cultural definitions of gender are not necessarily biblical categories. God's definitions of how men and women should act as gendered, created beings is often wider than the stipulations applied in human culture.

While God created all aspects of sex and gender to be good, the entrance of sin into creation distorted that inherent goodness. The ways we understand sex and gender have become confused. Instead of remembering that these good gifts are just aspects of godly human relationships designed to help us flourish as creatures and enjoy God's presence (Genesis 1:26–31), we often manipulate them to serve our own desires in a futile attempt to redefine our own identities.

Empathetically acknowledging brokenness through the counseling relationship

God designed Alex and Devin in his image. Our triune God, who lives in relationship, left no doubt that he wants those created in his image to live in relationship also. He declared it is not good for man to be alone. He wants us to be in relationship. However, since the first bite of the forbidden fruit, relationships have been corrupted.

Both Alex and Devin have had a tiny taste of what is good in relationships—affection, companionship, rapport, and solidarity. Of course they long for more of this, but they are looking to a false substitute for this sense of belonging and affirmation. The Lord wants our desire for companionship and acceptance to lead us to him. He wants us to taste and see that *he* is good.

Psalm 34:8–10 describes it this way:

> Oh, taste and see that the LORD is good!
>   Blessed is the man who takes refuge in him!
> Oh, fear the LORD, you his saints,
>   for those who fear him have no lack!
> The young lions suffer want and hunger;
>   but those who seek the Lord lack no good thing.

What a sweet promise for Alex and Devin. Their lives thus far have lacked so much, but as they turn to the Lord and give him their reverence (fear) they can move from a position of impoverishment to those who lack no good thing.

Alex and Devin need to know that God—the source of every good and perfect gift (James 1:17)—wants to be their friend. They also need to understand that Jesus suffered—was alienated, abandoned, bullied—and that he sees the pain they have endured and the ways they have sought to seek resolution to their loneliness and feelings of rejection.

Gaining the opportunity to unpack this with Alex and Devin will usually only happen after building a relationship with them, after you reflect God's love and concern for their suffering. Counseling children who self-identify as a sexual or gender minority involves unique challenges. Probably the most important challenge for the counselor to acknowledge up front is that the counselee is likely sitting in the counseling office only after having been brought there by a parent or sent there by a church pastor or youth director. Unlike typical adult counseling situations where the counselee realizes he or she has an unresolved issue and asks for help, most children presenting with LGBTQ+ identity or behavior are in counseling solely because they have been *told* by an adult that they need help. Consequently, counselors who work on these issues with minors will need to prayerfully gain the counselee's trust and move forward with a shared agenda. That agenda cannot be to change the child's orientation.

Many children who present with LGBTQ+ identity or behavior are experiencing (or have experienced) some sort of emotional trauma or persistent suffering that has led them to conclude that embracing LGBTQ+ identity or behavior will provide the safe refuge they seek. Perhaps sexual and gender confusion among children is prevalent today due to the internet, the rise and manipulative power of social media, and the cultural trend toward selfishness and self-preoccupation that results in more and more children experiencing suffering, early sexualization, and various kinds of abuse. In such difficult circumstances, children will seek comfort and security. Controlling one's sexual and gender identity and behaviors associated with those aspects of identity offer a sense of refuge in a turbulent and potentially harmful world.

Perhaps the trauma or suffering spoken of in the previous paragraph involves failed or disappointing peer relationships. Perhaps it involves bullying, harassment, or intimidation. Perhaps it involves chastisement or even verbally or emotionally abusive behavior from other adults, including parents. Perhaps it involves exposure to pornography, inappropriate touch, or even criminal sexual activity.

The counselor's first goal should be to establish a safe relationship with the counselee. Counselors can do that through asking the kinds of history-related questions that would uncover the source of trauma or suffering. Then counselors need to empathize with their young counselees, let them process those experiences and feelings, and bring them into the presence of our kind God, the defender of the weak (Psalm 72:12–13), the compassionate Father (Psalm 103:13), the One who brings justice to the oppressed (Psalm 10:17–18).

Aiming for the Heart

It is not only the environment around us that needs to be redeemed; we need to be redeemed from the brokenness that is inside of us. All of us have suffered and all of us have gone astray in our suffering (Isaiah 53:6). We have all turned to our own way—what we think is right and what we think will satisfy us. We all have desires battling within us (James 4:1) that drag us away from God and entice us toward sin and death (James 1:14–15). We need redemption at the heart level, not just in the environment around us.

As you read Alex's and Devin's stories you might have thought it would be relatively simple to find the core heart issue each young person struggles with. After all, Alex's transgender ideation is caused by his lack of proper integration into male peer social systems, right? And Devin suffered through a failure to bond with her mother. She wants to connect with other females, right?

It might be tempting to think at this point that a child like Alex struggles with gender identity because the desire for gender-related sin is in his heart. Or to assume that Devin struggles with same-sex attraction because that particular desire controls her heart.

Counselors, though, would be wise to avoid this kind of two-dimensional thinking. We live in three dimensions, and outward behavior doesn't always directly reflect the underlying heart cause—just as the image of the Wizard of Oz didn't much resemble the man behind the curtain. While some desires do have a direct correlation to their satisfying behavior (for instance, feeling thirsty leads one to take a drink of water), many do not.

One example is feeling lonely. One person might seek to satisfy that desire through calling a friend. But that isn't the only way to address loneliness. Others might also attempt to satisfy (or escape from) loneliness through engaging in social media, going to a public place to be around others, binge-watching television, playing video games, eating or drinking to excess, or watching pornography. Not all of these outward behaviors accurately identify the underlying desire (not being lonely). But they are all *possible* ways for a lonely person to respond to that desire to not feel alone.

Identifying the Core Issue—Idolatry

The real issue that children and young people need guidance to wrestle with is that of idolatry. A struggle or sin related to sex is never just a sexual problem. And struggle or sin related to gender is never simply a gender problem. This chapter is narrowly focused on sexual and gender-related issues, but Scripture tells us that idolatry is actually at the core of *all* struggles with *all* types of sin. Here's how James describes idolatry and its role in our sinful behavior:

But each person is tempted when he is lured and enticed by his own desire. Then desire when it has conceived gives birth to sin, and sin when it is fully grown brings forth death. (1:14–15)

The "desire" James cites is more of a *controlling desire*, one that has become too important or is disproportionately powerful. Such desires wind up leading to sin, as James says, because we *want* to satisfy them so badly that when temptation comes along and promises relief to our longing, we jump at the chance.

So what kinds of desires are typically involved when a child struggles with same-sex attraction or gender identity? The following diagram represents typical desires that become too important and wind up capturing hearts and controlling behavior:

How Desires Become Idols

Love
Good self-image
Affirmation
Affection
Security
No pain or suffering
Control
Comfort
Understanding
Intimacy

Disappointment
Discouragement
Despair

"I must have this...I don't care what it takes"

Desire → Idol

The desires that often capture our hearts and become idols are generally benign[5]. They're desires like the ones mentioned in the preceding diagram—desires for such things as affirmation, affection, control, and comfort. And, we should note that these desires, in their proper context, are generally good or at least benign. In their proper contexts, they're all part of who we are, created as God's image-bearers.

In a fallen world, we don't bear God's image as intended. Our hearts are as fallen and as deceitful as every other part of creation that has been subjected to the effects of the Fall into sin. Consequently, our desires can grow into idols as we experience the desire and then find exactly how difficult it is to satisfy. When we wish to feel more affirmation (or any of the other desires listed in the diagram), we are often disappointed because others don't adequately provide the satisfaction of that desire. Sometimes we are disappointed because we desire those things too much, or in their own particular way, or in measure inconsistent with God's good provision for us. Sin affects the fulfillment of our desires by either preventing them from being satisfied or causing us to selfishly inflate the extent to which we want them satisfied.

As we sit with disappointment, we stew, become angry, and likely experience even greater disappointment as the desire goes unmet time and again. Eventually that disappointment grows into desperation. And we say something to the effect of, "I need this desire met. I don't care what it takes." At that point the otherwise good desire has evolved into an idol. Now we are willing to sacrifice anything in order to meet the desire.

The work of the counselor, therefore, is threefold.

- *First*, it's important to acknowledge the suffering that is present.

- *Second,* while acknowledging the suffering, we also need to help the child or young person understand the particular idolatry at work beneath the surface, driving the behavior and leading to prolonged suffering.
- *Third,* we need to compassionately help that young image-bearer progressively walk in his or her union with Christ and in the grace they receive through God's love.

Walking in Grace Is Necessary

The beginning step of walking in grace is repentance. Repentance is the biblical response to all sin and the idolatry that drives it. To facilitate this, counselors and parents need to focus on two things:

- Helping children and young people to understand their union with Christ
- Helping them to find contentment in Christ, rather than in their circumstances

Why do I say this?

Scripture tells us that clinging to God is the source of all good and right desire-related fulfillment. The psalmist says in Psalm 37:4: "Delight yourself in the LORD, and he will give you the desires of your heart." In the Sermon on the Mount Jesus exhorts his hearers, "But seek first the kingdom of God and his righteousness, and all these things will be added to you" (Matthew 6:33). In both instances, the order of operations is clear: God wants us to trust, love, and rest in him *first,* and then from him we find the right satisfaction of our desires.

For Alex, as we glean data from his story and use the categories of desire in the model above, we might learn that Alex wrestles with idols of affirmation, positive self-image, and comfort. It would be important to talk with Alex, get to know his struggles, and ask him many questions. Then, an essential aspect of helping Alex walk in grace would be helping him understand the specific ways in which God affirms him as a dearly loved son and as a young man. Take Alex directly to God's Word, and help him to wrestle with what God says about who he is and the character of God's love for him. Some Scripture suggestions for Alex might include the following: Psalms 71:3; 73:23; 139:13–16; Jeremiah 29:11, and 2 Corinthians 4:7–18. Each of these passages speaks about how God's Word shines light into the particular darkness that Alex experiences.

Only when Alex rests in what God says about him can he stop trying to satisfy those desires through his behavior and using his behavior to manipulate other people. Only by resting in the ultimate comfort that comes through the finished work of Christ on his behalf can Alex stop trying to escape his own discomfort through identifying himself to be "Alexis"—an identity that lacks all of the suffering that Alex struggles with in the real world.

Or, consider Devin. Perhaps she's wrestling with idols of intimacy, being understood, and affection. Only through actively resting in the intimacy she receives through her relationship with the Lord can Devin stop trying to create that intimacy in the embrace of someone else. Only through faith in the fact that the Lord knows her and loves her completely can Devin relinquish her feverish search to be understood by another, in place of the parents and grandparents whom she feels never understood her. Only through experiencing the ultimate affection of God, who calls her "Daughter," and Jesus, who calls her "Sister," will Devin stop looking for substitute affection from others.

As with Alex, take Devin to God's Word and help her to consider what God says about his actual, faithful covenant love for her. Some passages that might be helpful include Psalm 91:14–15; Isaiah 43:1–5; 2 Corinthians 6:18; and Hebrews 2:10–18.

Walking in Grace Involves Change

Genuine repentance means going in a new direction—toward God and away from your own way. So it's a lifelong process that happens through discipleship. It involves growing in the understanding and experience of one's union with Christ and all of the identity-related power that being grafted into God's family brings. It also involves practical discipleship—practical help—in finding contentment in Christ, rather than in circumstances. That happens through patient, careful, and compassionate discipleship.

Discipleship is a team sport. Alex and Devin, and others in similar situations, need older, more mature disciples (counselors, parents, mentors) to help them learn and relearn to experience daily the truth, power, and benefits of union with Christ. We all need others to help us exercise self-control. Just as Paul describes in Ephesians 4:11–16, we are all part of one Body, and we are called to use our various gifts in "speaking the truth in love" to one another on an ongoing basis. Only through this intensive, lifelong, deliberate, love-motivated discipleship will the individual members of the Body mature.

And we need to remember that the process of growing in maturity is gradual, progressive, and sometimes painfully slow and fraught with setbacks. God provides grace for counselors and their young counselees in all of those difficult places.

This ongoing process could look like a counselor compassionately naming the counselee's uncovered idols in each conversation and asking two questions:

- "Where have you struggled recently with (this idol)?"
- "What can you do to remember what God's Word says when (this idol) comes up again?"

In other words, the counselor is graciously asking the counselee to map out his or her recent experience and to prepare for similar spiritual battle in the future. In neither instance should the counselor condemn, but rather, he should ask the counselee to consider how he or she might believe and act differently, if they increasingly rest in God's Word.

One other practical way counselors might help young people learn to walk in grace is to model social skills or facilitate social situations with which the child or teen struggles. Modeling or role-playing appropriate ways to express disappointment, fear, anger, or other emotions is important for those who have never learned these skills. This might include evaluating current practices with the young person and formulating strategies to reframe, modify, or terminate unsafe or unhealthy relationships with particular peers.

And, of course, counselors should always assess the presence of or prospect of immediate danger for the young people they counsel. Children and young people who self-identify as same-sex attracted or trans are bullied at far higher rates than their peers, and they participate in self-harming behaviors at far higher rates than peers. If you believe the child is in imminent danger, involve the appropriate authorities, drive them to the emergency room, or call 911 immediately.

A Word to Parents

More and more parents are finding they have an Alex or a Devin in their family. Much of what has been written for counselors in this chapter can be readily applied to a parent-child relationship—particularly the information on suffering, idolatry, and discipleship. There are additional ways parents can help their children who self-identify as LGBTQ+ or struggle with sexual or gender identity issues.

First, take steps to actively and repeatedly assess the potential for bullying. Regularly monitor your child's social media accounts, texts, and online activity. Ask questions about anything that seems potentially harmful. Look for nonverbal cues from your child that something is wrong. Is your child becoming more withdrawn? Does he or she seem to have less interest in favorite activities? Has his or her appearance changed? Are his or her grades suddenly worse? Any of these cues could be signs that your child feels under threat. Prayerfully and compassionately ask your child about what you notice. Children will generally not want to talk about perceived threats for a variety of reasons. Be patient and persistent, and be willing to talk with other adults (i.e., teachers, parents of friends, etc.) who might have knowledge about a situation that needs to be addressed.

Second, regularly, throughout your child's stages of development, have frank, proactive, and age-appropriate conversations with your child about God's good design for sex, sexuality, and gender.[6] As soon as your child is able to comprehend gender differences (usually around the age of two to three), begin to talk with your child about how God created them male or female for a reason—and that those distinctions are good, permanent gifts from God. Particularly as children enter elementary school, begin to talk appropriately about the gift of sex and sexuality, and the context within which God created it to bless his people and honor him. The culture around them will not hesitate to introduce these topics early on, so children need a biblical lens for evaluating the world's ideology.

Ask your child how they experience being made male or female. What does it mean to them? Do they think they are the "right kind" of boy or girl? What disappointments, fears, and misgivings do they experience? How do they feel they fail to measure up to others' expectations (primarily, your own)? How do they struggle with envy because others around them seem to be "better" boys or girls than they are? Engage your child around these areas. Don't be afraid to hear your child say hard things. If there are questions you feel you can't answer, seek out other people or resources to help. And, remember, you're responsible to keep the conversation going. Don't let it stop as your child gets older or seems uncomfortable.

Third, prayerfully, actively, and purposefully engage your child in conversation about what they've seen, heard, and experienced. Disciple them to interpret and judge these things from a biblical perspective. Ask your child how he or she has interpreted and interacted with sexual and sexualized images that they've seen online or in other media. Ask them what their friends think about these issues. Ask them frankly how they're processing their own sexual desire. In all cases, compassionately hold up Scripture as the sole authority on sexual and gender identity. By discussing these issues with your child, help them become wise and discerning.

Fourth, ask your child if he or she has ever experienced same-sex attraction or has wrestled with his or her gender. If they respond that they have, don't panic. Experiencing such thoughts and asking such questions is not unusual in a fallen world. Engage your child in a dialogue about their questions. Reassure them of your love. Demonstrate that you are willing to walk alongside them and help them wrestle through these deep and significant questions. Also, help your child challenge the worldly wisdom that the experience of same-sex attraction equals a gay or lesbian identity. That simply isn't true. Many people experience at least some same-sex attraction. Most don't act on it or identify as gay or lesbian.

There are many excellent resources available to parents to help children and young people navigate these deep waters of the heart.[7] What is most important for your child is that you remain present and engaged with them throughout this process. Don't avoid it because it seems too difficult. Don't refuse to discuss it with your child because you think it will simply go away. Don't allow the competing narrative from either the fallen culture or your child's fallen and utterly deceitful heart to be the only voice your child listens to. Take up the spiritual weapons that are yours in Christ to defend your child (2 Corinthians 10:3–5).

Fifth, if your child does struggle with same-sex attraction or gender identity, remember that such struggles are not always lifelong, nor do they need to be life-dominating. A person who gets to the point of either struggling with these issues or self-identifying as LGBTQ+ has typically been wrestling with these questions, desires, and disappointments for years. If the Lord brings change, it will most likely be gradual and progressive. Remember, discipleship is the core of the process of helping sexual or gender strugglers, and discipleship is a lifelong process. Don't become discouraged yourself. Don't become discouraged if your child continues to struggle or experience temptation to sin. Walk with them compassionately, speaking the truth in love, and help them gradually put sin to death in their body while finding their true and lasting identity in Christ.

Sixth, pray with and for your child. There's nothing more important you can do for him or her. Pray proactively for him or her, that the Lord would shield them from lies and deceptions rooted in evil and meant to lead them astray. Pray also that your child would know how to respond to images, messages, and worldviews that seem good, but are in reality contrary to Scripture. Pray that the Lord himself would keep them from giving in to the self-centered worldview that says one's only hope is to find maximum happiness and personal satisfaction.

Through all of these circumstances, it is essential to know that the Lord loves our children more than we do. He is committed to working for their good and their holiness. Trust him to work in them, and through you, to accomplish that.

CHAPTER 13
HELPING CHILDREN WHO SELF-HARM
CHARLES HODGES

Angie was seventeen when her family brought her to me for help. She was struggling with suicidal thinking, substance abuse, and cutting. Angie came from a blended home in which her mother, stepfather, and siblings all considered themselves Christian. They attended a church that believed and taught the Bible. They had regular family devotions, and her parents honestly believed they were doing their best to guide their family in a godly direction.

Angie's behavior problems started at age fourteen. Her mother thought it was a mixture of adolescent rebellion enhanced by the absence of her biological father. Her father had abandoned the family when Angie was seven, leaving a large hole in her life. Like many children from families divided by divorce, she blamed herself. *If I had just been better*, she thought, *none of this would have happened.*

When she was around the age of nine, her mother remarried, and for a while, her stepfather's presence seemed to bring calm to Angie's life. However, things went sideways when Angie hit thirteen. Angie began to view her stepfather as an enemy. Together, Angie's mother and stepfather tried to control her behavior. They read every helpful book on teenagers and their rebellion they could find, but the harder they worked at it, the more she rebelled.

They removed everything in her life that was an opportunity for her to rebel in a destructive way. They turned off her internet access, believing that she was on forums or message boards that encouraged her troublesome behavior. They made it nearly impossible for her to meet with friends, who seemed frightening at best and opportunities for drug use and sexual immorality at worst. They decided to move her from her public school to home to finish her schooling.

By the time I met her the only thing she believed could help her to calm the raging fear and sadness in her life was cutting herself with something sharp. When the blood flowed, she had a sense of exhilaration and then calm that nothing else could deliver. She hid her cutting from her mom and stepdad, but one day, a sibling saw the cuts and scars and told her mom. Her parents were devastated and had no idea where to turn next. They had been in counseling with Angie for a year, and now they were at their wits' end.

As a result of her encounters with the counselor recommended by their pediatrician, Angie had a diagnosis of non-suicidal self-injury or NSSI. She struggled with a depressed mood and at times with anxiety. She had been in counseling for a year without a significant change in her mood or her behavior.

On arrival, Angie received a physical exam from a nurse at our counseling center that documented her self-injury. There were scars on her upper arms, thighs, and wrists. They were thin straight scars that could have been made by a razor blade or box cutter. Around her wrist was an elastic band that she snapped whenever there was conflict. In counseling she told us it was a substitute for cutting herself. She said it reduced the tension she often felt and helped her feel better.

Angie's story is not unusual. Approximately 6 to 7 percent of people between the ages of eleven and eighty resort to some form of self-harm. The current medical definition specifies injuring themselves in some non-fatal way without any suicidal intent five times in the last year. They do it to relieve anxiety or depression resulting from difficulties with relationships, negative thinking, and disturbing thoughts.[1]

Those who self-harm do not come from a specific race, socioeconomic status, gender, or country. NSSI is not unique to developed industrial nations. Individuals usually start the practice between age eleven and fifteen, but some as late as age sixty. Most people who self-injure have other emotional struggles. They carry labels that include eating disorders, depression, anxiety, PTSD, and substance abuse disorders.[2] When asked what the goal of NSSI is for them, usually they say they want to feel better.

How does causing significant pain make one feel better about the problems of life? It is difficult to say exactly what the mechanism is, but there has been considerable speculation that the relief associated with self-harm is similar to the effect that running has on runners. Our bodies have a natural means of dealing with pain and stress by releasing substances called endorphins into our circulation. Those endorphins reduce the discomfort and make the stress and pain bearable. Those of us who run are familiar with the "runner's high" and miss it when we cannot run. It may be that a similar physical process draws those who self-harm back to it.

Where to Start?

Where do we start with the child or adolescent who is cutting, and what are our goals as we counsel them? The following are things we have found important in helping those who self-harm.

Listening

Listening long and well is very important when faced with a child who is suffering enough to harm themselves. In that moment, careful, quiet listening with a non-judgmental, unshockable attitude will give the child the opportunity to tell you what is at the heart of their suffering. Proverbs 18:13 tells us that we would be unwise to give an answer to a problem without hearing the whole of it. I cannot emphasize too much how important this is. If you want to help, you must start by listening.

Start with good questions and then keep listening: When did this begin? What was happening the first time you cut yourself? What about the next time? Keep asking questions. As you listen, keep in mind that it is not likely this problem will be solved in a day. While it might seem obvious that any parent would want us to tell their child to stop and give a hundred reasons why, it is more important to get to the heart of their suffering.

There will be a cause, and if you listen long enough, they will tell you. At times, part of good listening involves asking good questions that open the conversation to talking about hard subjects. For Angie, like most of us, a combination of hard things led her to cutting.

The loss of connection to her biological father loomed large in her life. Like many young children, Angie blamed herself for her father's leaving. It placed her at risk for other significant problems. While her stepfather was a godly man who worked hard at helping, there was no answer that could satisfy Angie when she declared, "You are not my father."

Many of those who self-harm have been victims of school bullying. Others have been sexually or physically abused by adults who should have protected them. Social media has become a dual problem. It provides information about self-harm and the opportunity to be bullied on the internet. Both can contribute to the problem. So listen for the suffering that the child in front of you has encountered. Knowing what lies beneath their behavior will help you apply the comfort of the gospel.

Taking Strugglers to Jesus

A good friend of mine once said that when we encounter people who are struggling in life, we should take them to Jesus. Jesus cares about them and their suffering. Depending on the age of the struggler, there are many good Scriptures that apply. For the younger, the invitation that Jesus offers in Matthew 19:13–15 (NASB) is a good place to begin: "Then some children were brought to Him so that He might lay His hands on them and pray; and the disciples rebuked them. But Jesus said, 'Let the children alone, and do not hinder them from coming to Me; for the kingdom of heaven belongs to such as these.' After laying His hands on them, He departed from there."

The adults with Jesus didn't think that children and their problems mattered, but Jesus said, "Let the children come to me." As we seek to help the young person who is self-harming, we must show them Jesus. He is not absent; he is present and actively interested in them and their problems.

The young person who is struggling needs to see that Jesus is prepared to help them. As he said, "Come to me, all who labor and are weary and heavy laden, and I will give you rest. Take my yoke upon you, and learn from me, for I am gentle and lowly in heart, and you will find rest for your souls. For my yoke is easy, and my burden is light." (Matthew 11:28–30) Whatever the problem is that drives them to self-harm, our Lord offers to take that burden and give them rest.

The rest that Jesus offers would give Angie relief from the burdens she carried. It would last much longer than the temporary surge of endorphins she might get from cutting herself. That rest would come from changing the story she had attached to her abandonment by her father. Her seven-year-old mind reasoned that she must be to blame. Further, she believed that any future relationship or friendship would suffer the same fate. She was left without the understanding or tools to face the ups and downs of life. Eventually self-harm filled that void as a way to punish herself, have control over things that felt out of control, and numb emotional pain.

In order for Angie, and others like her, to find rest the story had to change. Every time she thought of her father, she blamed herself. She was not worthy of being loved and she had no reason to think that any relationship in the future would be different. It took time, but as we talked she came to understand that as a believer in Christ, God saw her as chosen, holy, and beloved (Colossians 3:12). Her father did not abandon the family because she was a bad person. He left for reasons that had nothing to do with her. She needed to learn that all future relationships would not end the same way. And gradually she came to see that what God said about her and her relationships was true and trustworthy.

She learned about trust from the letter the apostle Paul wrote to the believers at Rome. From chapter 8 she learned that she was not condemned for the behavior of others. She could see she was a child of God and that in difficult times the Holy Spirit was praying for her as she struggled. She learned that God intended to use the experiences in her life to shape her into the image of Jesus, which would be for her good. She also learned that nothing in life or on earth would ever separate her from the love of God.

In counseling Angie was encouraged to remind herself of the gospel promises from Romans 8. Much has been written and said about preaching the gospel to ourselves in difficult times. Angie was encouraged to rehearse the biblical principles from Romans in the order they are written in the chapter whenever she was inclined to self-harm. This helped her change the story.

Angie also took great comfort from seeing how Jesus cared for Martha, Mary, and Lazarus. John 11 gives us an amazing picture of how much God and his Son Jesus cares for us in the middle of our suffering. She came to understand that Jesus knew all about the illness and suffering of Lazarus (v. 4), and that he had a plan for it (v. 7). Angie saw that Jesus cared deeply for Martha, Mary, and Lazarus. Despite the fact that Jesus knew he would be raising Lazarus from the dead in a few minutes, when confronted with Mary and Martha and their friends weeping, Jesus wept (v. 35). It gave Angie comfort and confidence that just as Jesus knew, planned, cared, and acted for Lazarus, he would do the same for her.

There are many passages in the Psalms that offer comfort to the sufferer. Psalm 13 also became a favorite for Angie. It begins with a lament. "How long, O Lord? Will you forget me forever? How long will You hide Your face from me? How long shall I take counsel in my soul, Having sorrow in my heart all the day? How long will my enemy be exalted over me?" (vv. 1–2 NASB). In the end, the writer says, "But I have trusted in your lovingkindness; My heart shall rejoice in Your salvation. I will sing to the LORD, because he has dealt bountifully with me" (vv. 5–6). These verses told Angie the truth that God intends to take care of her through all of her struggles.

There are many characters in the Bible who are good examples of those who suffered and the care God gave them through it. Joseph, Hannah, David, Daniel (and his three friends), all faced suffering while their lives reflected God's care for them. Angie found encouragement as we talked about their stories.

Eventually, as counseling progressed, the story that helped Angie the most was about our Lord Jesus Christ, the one who became like us so he can sympathize with us. We went over Hebrews 4:14–16 many times.

> Since we have a great high priest who has passed through the heavens, Jesus the Son of God, let us hold fast our confession. For we do not have a high priest who cannot sympathize with our weaknesses, but One who has been tempted in all things as we are, yet without sin. Therefore let us draw near with confidence to the throne of grace, so that we may receive mercy and find grace to help in time of need. (NASB)

As Angie struggled, she took to heart the invitation in this passage to go to Jesus to receive mercy and find grace to help her in her struggles.

Angie was introduced to the gospel through the suffering and sympathy of Jesus for her. While she came from a Christian home, she was uncertain about her faith. That is not unusual for those who struggle with self-harm. This seems to be a common response for individuals when they participate in a behavior they feel must be hidden or of which they are ashamed. It does not change their state of grace, but it does affect their confidence in it. As we reflected together on how Jesus was "a man of sorrows acquainted with grief" and that he bore her sins, the gospel she had accepted as a child became alive to her.

The gospel is essential to any counseling that will result in meaningful lasting change. The apostle Paul says in 2 Corinthians 5:17 (NASB), "If anyone is in Christ, he is a new creature; the old things passed away; behold, new things have come." Because of the gospel I could assure Angie that she could grow and change and become more like Christ. I could share with her that God would be working in her both to will and to do his good pleasure (Philippians 2:13). The gospel encouraged Angie in her struggle against self-harm. She could do "all things through him who gave her strength" (Philippians 4:13).

Stopping the Harm

While Angie was not being actively harmed by anyone, that cannot be said of many of those who choose to self-harm. Many who self-harm are sexually and physically abused. They self-harm in the hope that someone will notice and intervene. Others are bullied at school or on social media. No matter what the nature of the harm or who the perpetrator is, when it comes to the attention of the counselor, it should stop. Whatever appropriate steps or reporting are required to stop the harm should be carried out as soon as possible. This would include reporting any activity believed to be illegal to appropriate authorities. In most states, counselors are mandated to report physical or sexual abuse of children, and they should do so promptly.

Changing Goals

A wise pediatrician once told me to never ask a teenager why they did something. He said they would just look at you and say, "I don't know." Instead, he suggests we ask, "What was your goal?" He was correct that this question usually gets a more detailed answer (and it works equally well with adults). When I asked Angie what her goal was during cutting, she told me it relieved her tension and made her feel better.

While her goal was a little more complicated than that, it provided a starting point for discussion and illustrated a problem she faced. Angie needed to change her goal. The primary goal for all believers is found in 2 Corinthians 5:9 (NASB) where it says, "Therefore also we have as our ambition, whether at home or absent, to be pleasing to him." Our goal is to glorify God with our lives, and to love him with all our hearts, souls, and minds (Matthew 22:37–39). That love is meant to drive us to obey him (John 14:21) and to serve others (John 13). If Angie were going to escape the slavery of self-harm, she was going to have to start by choosing a new goal.

Choosing to Trust Our Savior

Paul speaks of the choice before Angie in Romans 6:16 where he says, "Do you not know that if you present yourselves to anyone as obedient slaves, you are slaves of the one whom you obey, either of sin, which leads to death, or of obedience, which leads to righteousness?" There are lots of ways to deal with the struggles and suffering that life presents. Angie was using self-harm to deal with the pain of her father's leaving. But the good news is Christians are not obligated to deal with the problems of life in destructive ways. We get to choose who we will serve. For Angie, this meant she could deal with her suffering in ways that did not include cutting herself. For many like her it means they will choose to deal with their pain and suffering biblically. The advantage to the believer is that it is God who is at work in us both to will and to do his good pleasure (Philippians 2:13). Whatever God requires of us, he will make us able to do (Philippians 4:13).

Responding biblically takes away the need for self-harm. This is not to make it sound easy to simply replace destructive ways to deal with pain with biblical ways. For Angie worry and fear were part of her struggle. Those who need a solution to their worry and fear find a place to look for comfort and guidance from Paul as he wrote to the Philippians.

> Rejoice in the Lord always; again, I will say, rejoice! Let your gentle spirit be known to all men. The Lord is near. Be anxious for nothing, but in everything by prayer and supplication with thanksgiving let your requests be made known to God. And the peace of God, which surpasses all comprehension, will guard your hearts and your minds in Christ Jesus. (Philippians 4:4–7 NASB)

This is a passage filled with hope for Angie and others who self-harm. While Paul sat in prison facing certain death, he told us that we can change our mood. Instead of seeing life—and our suffering—as a catastrophe, we can respond with joy because Jesus is near us as we struggle. Paul goes further to tell us that we can choose not to worry. Instead we can pray and ask for a better to solution to the problems that are the source of our anxiety. The outcome is peace instead of the momentary relief found in self-harm.

Trust is the polar opposite of worry and fear. Those who self-harm need to grow in trusting God if they hope to escape it. Solomon wisely advised us to "Trust in the LORD with all your heart and do not lean on your own understanding. In all your ways acknowledge Him, and He will make your paths straight" (Proverbs 3:5–6 NASB). Instead of depending on her own interpretation of life that led her to self-harm, Angie would now put her trust in God and his Word.

Hoping for Change

Those who self-harm need you to give them real, gospel-based hope that they won't have to keep cutting to deal with the unpleasant realities of their lives. Paul offers this hope and a pattern for change in his letter to the Ephesians. He says that as believers we can "put off your old self, which belongs to your former manner of life and is corrupt through deceitful desires, and to be renewed in the spirit of your minds, and to put on the new self, created after the likeness of God in true righteousness and holiness" (Ephesians 4:22–24).

This process of change has come to be called progressive sanctification. The very thought that we can change and that God is at the heart of it, can give hope to those who self-harm.

Gaining a biblical understanding of guilt and shame can result in lasting relief from troublesome emotions that self-harm cannot give. Paul tells us if we are in Christ, old things are passing away and new things are coming (2 Corinthians 5:17). Angie would not be identified for the rest of her life as a "cutter." She did not need to feel shame for sins Jesus had forgiven. Instead she would be able to use her experiences to help others who struggled as she once did. She could comfort others with the comfort with which she had been comforted.

Learning to deal with anger over past hurts and the desire to get even with those who hurt us can change how we see adverse events in the future. It is very important for those who struggle as Angie did to learn to deal with their anger in way that honors God. As much as she blamed herself, at other times she seethed with anger toward her father, which ended up being displaced on those around her. She found Paul's instruction very helpful, when he told the Roman Christians to never take their own revenge (Romans 12:19–21). Instead, she learned to make room for God's judgment. God would take care of all the getting even that needed to be done. Instead of being overcome by evil, Angie could work at repaying the evil done to her with good.

Eventually, gratitude frees us from bitterness. On a bad day I heard a preacher on the radio say, "It's time for you to stop counting your bruises and start counting your blessings." As that helped me, it also helped Angie. At some point, if we are going to glorify our God, then we have to be willing to thank him for the care he gives us. Paul, sitting in prison, told the Ephesian church, that they should be "always giving thanks for all things in the name of our Lord Jesus Christ, to God even the Father" (Ephesians 5:20). Angie did the hard work of focusing her attention on what God was doing for her now, and not past hurts.

Seeing Trials as God Sees Them

It was important in the process of counseling for Angie to see trials the way God sees them. Her counseling started in Psalm 13 and moved through the struggles that Joseph suffered. Joseph's words in Genesis 50:20 came to mean a great deal to her. "You meant it for evil, God meant it for good . . . " would become the prelude to her introduction to Paul's statement in Romans 8:28–29: "And we know that for those who love God all things work together for good, for those who are called according to his purpose. For those whom he foreknew he also predestined to be conformed to the image of his Son, in order that he might be the firstborn among many brothers."

Angie moved from seeing every adversity as a cause for self-harm, to seeing God's care for her in her suffering, to understand Jesus as a fellow sufferer, and to trust that God was working in her life to shape her into the image of Christ.

Taking Thoughts Captive

An important part of Angie's growth was helping her to think differently in real time as she faced real struggles. It was a daily exercise of changing her thinking about a variety of things some of which would result in her considering self-harm. Angie learned to "take her thoughts captive" as Paul wrote in 2 Corinthians 10:5. The process involved confronting disturbing, sometimes sinful thinking and putting biblical principals in its place. It required memorizing Scripture and replacing self-harm with normal productive activity. This included a wide range of activities, including physical exercise and chores around the house. Instead of ruminating on hurts and eventually cutting to relieve the stress, Angie worked her way through a succession of biblical principles and memorized verses, such as the ones we have discussed, that would often end in Christian service to another struggler.

A Word to Parents

Most parents experience at least one shocking discovery about one or more of their children. Life is going along as well as can be expected and with a blinding flash and deafening roar trouble strikes. When that happens, it's easy to lose your bearings and to react with fear and anger to the trouble you see in front of you. But when you discover that your child is self-harming, remember at that moment in time, you will be your child's first counselor. Whether you wish to or not makes no difference. The option before you is to either occupy that role as best you can by God's grace, or to do poorly by responding with all your fear, hurt, and disappointment in plain view. You get one opportunity in that moment to respond in a helpful, biblical way. Start with asking God to help you and then listen to your child.

Next, remember that you don't have to face this alone. In trying to fix this problem by yourself, you may miss the helpful resources that God has placed around you. Your church, your pastor, a counselor who will minister to your child and your family, your friends who will pray for you, are all allies in the battle for your child. Enlist them at your earliest opportunity!

Keep in mind that all change in life is an ongoing process. Paul spoke often of putting off the old man and putting on the new (Ephesians 4:22–24). At no time did he say that the coming change would be quick, easy, and painless. For parents this is probably the hardest part. A child who has spent years working their way into the problem will also take a good bit of time to escape. Parents must be willing to live with their child on the schedule that God has arranged. Of all things a parent can do, praying for their child is one of the most important. James tells us that the effectual fervent prayer of a righteous man or woman can accomplish much (James 5:16).

As you pray and wait, never lose sight in the middle of your struggle that God intends to use it for your good and his glory. He will use it to make you more like his Son Jesus. And God our Father promises never to abandon you in the process.

COUNSELING CHILDREN WITH A DISEASE

JONI AND FRIENDS

No detail was missed. Pink balloons—check. Unicorn cake—check. Presents—oh yes! Everyone worked hard to give Stella the party of her dreams. Squeals and giggles could be heard down the hall, and in case anyone was unclear, a sign proclaiming, "Happy 9th Birthday, Stella!" left a trail of glitter to her door.

Stella's mom delighted at seeing her nine-year-old girl's grin, and she knew the party was a welcome distraction for all the patients. But she also saw Stella's strength waning after only fifteen minutes. The guests, some younger and some older, understood when the party had to end early because they too were in various phases of treatment. Cancer doesn't go away for birthdays.

Stella was a vibrant, feisty third-grader when she started experiencing dizziness and fainting at school. "I didn't think in a million years that it would be something serious," her mother Kami said. "We almost didn't even take her to the pediatrician right away because she was so healthy and active. After a few days I did start to worry, but I still never expected to hear the word *cancer*."

Doctors discovered Stella's white blood count was six times higher than normal, and their family's battle with leukemia began. It was three years of inpatient and outpatient treatment, experimenting with different medicines to help her tiny body survive both the cancer and the chemo. Stella lost her bouncy blonde curls and half her body weight.

A Foundation of Hope

When a child is diagnosed with a chronic illness there are the initial challenges of adjusting to the demands of the condition and treatments. Treatment plans will likely require adjustments, especially if the illness leads to more losses, which may include disability, or even early death. Even as some face unimaginable pain and suffering, biblical counseling can help them continue to trust in God's goodness.

God's Word can be a solid foundation for children and families who sometimes feel like they're standing on shifting sands. Often, the children and their parents face isolation as friends and family struggle to know what to say or how to comfort them. Children may need to be kept out of school and regular activities for their own protection or to seek treatments.

Since the cheerleading program didn't begin until the fourth grade at Stella's school, she had held onto hope that she might be well enough to participate. Stella had dreamed of being a cheerleader since she was a toddler mimicking the cheerleaders on the sidelines of her brother's football games. She had hovered behind them in her pigtails, shouting along with every chant and even had a matching uniform complete with pom-poms. But as the summer tryouts neared, it was obvious that Stella would not have the strength. Stella started to spend more and more time in her room. Kami vacillated between reminding her daughter that she was lucky to be alive and undergoing such life-saving treatment—and curling up behind her as both their tears soaked Stella's pillowcase.

As a counselor, you can help the children and their parents think through any developmental milestones that will be delayed, or missed altogether, and how to process those losses. You can help them understand that their disappointment or even anger and frustration are natural responses.

A Facebook post from a mother of a child with cancer provides a glimpse into their tough reality.

"What You Don't See" by Rachel O'Neil

> You don't see the loneliness of a child not at school.
>
> You don't see the heartbreak as lifelong friends stop answering their calls.
>
> You don't see the sadness of a child who can't play outside.
>
> You don't see the pain when they miss the latest event or outing.
>
> You don't see the embarrassment when the appearance has changed and the hair disappears.
>
> You don't see the resignation in their eyes when the next round of vomiting, seizures & problems begin.
>
> You don't see the exhaustion so severe they no longer cry at the pain.
>
> You don't see the sheer hard work when they have to catch up.
>
> You don't see the devastation and loss at sudden new and lifelong disabilities.

You don't see the tears, the isolation, the depression, the
desolate, brutal destruction of that child with cancer . . .
day after relentless day . . . [1]

The truth is we can't see or even begin to understand the
full experiences of children with chronic illness or life-threatening diseases. But we can point them to Matthew 10:29–31
and Jesus's words that explain how God sees every single moment and counts every hair on their heads.

What is the price of two sparrows—one copper coin?
But not a single sparrow can fall to the ground without
your Father knowing it. And the very hairs on your head
are all numbered. So don't be afraid; you are more valuable to God than a whole flock of sparrows. (NLT)

Help the child understand Jesus's message about God's
love for us through the example of his tender care for these
common birds and his emphasis on how precious we are to
God. Children may wonder why God would let such a terrible
thing happen to them if he cares so much. An explanation of
sin and its impact on every aspect of our broken world may be
warranted, but more than anything these children are looking
for assurances that God loves them and sees their struggles.

Ask the child whether he or she has a scrapbook or a baby
book? You could also bring in your own or one belonging to a
family member for illustrative purposes. Ask the child if they
understand what a scrapbook is, explaining that we keep special mementos or keepsakes because they are very dear to us.
For example, you might save a first-place ribbon from a Field
Day event, or a mother may save the hair from her baby's first

haircut. God tells us that he cares so deeply about our pain and suffering that he keeps track of every tear.

> You keep track of all my sorrows.
> You have collected all my tears in your bottle.
> You have recorded each one in your book.
> Psalm 56:8 (NLT)

A Commitment to Learn about Specific Needs

Colin Mattoon is an associate pastor and hospice chaplain whose wife was diagnosed with autoimmune diseases. He's written resources to equip biblical counselors to help those with chronic illnesses, much of which can also apply to children. He says this counseling requires a commitment from counselors to learn about their patients' specific needs because they vary based on the different struggles and whether they also have disabilities.

"You may not know much about chronic illness or what struggles the chronically ill experience. However, if you keep asking questions, listen well, and work to understand their illness and the experience of the illness, this will not be a problem for long," Colin said.[2] "One thing you can do is say what facts and feelings you hear them expressing. For example, you could say, 'It sounds like you are feeling really sad about the way your disease is preventing you from doing X.'

"Another thing you can do is say what you think about their sadness. For example, you could say, 'I am sorry you are going through this right now. It just sounds really difficult and saddening to be going through X.' As you listen to the person, encourage them to be honest about their feelings."[3]

Collin emphasizes that feelings will change based on the illness, and, although a diagnosis predicts what these children can expect in the future, it's still hard to deal with the progression and loss. He suggests using King David's Psalm 13 as an example of someone calling out to God through their struggles.

On the day of her diagnosis, Kristin Hamer remembers facing her progressive eye disease with the innocent optimism of an eight-year-old, as she assured her mother that she'd get new eyes in heaven one day. But as she entered the challenging teen years, Kristin didn't want to feel different from other kids and didn't like the extra attention so she tried to hide her vision loss.

"I wish I could say that I kept that childlike faith and joy as my vision began to fade," Kristin said. "As I got into middle school and into high school, I really was not happy with the fact that I was different. I hated my disability and I tried everything I could to be as normal as possible. I did not want to be associated with people with disabilities because I didn't want to be different. I didn't want people to stare at me or to think that I was strange or odd. I didn't want people to feel sorry for me and to pity me. When you look at me, you cannot tell that I have a visual impairment, so I used that to my advantage."[4]

Kristin held on to her faith, but she struggled to understand God's ways.

Why did he create her with a genetic eye disease?
Why didn't God heal her?
What was her purpose?

Kristin's confidence grew during her college years as she learned to advocate for herself and help others. She heard Joni Eareckson Tada speak during a mission conference at the university and sensed God calling her to work with people affected by disability.

"Through this turning point, my loss of sight began to give me spiritual vision," Kristin explained. "In 2 Corinthians 12, Paul asked God to take away a thorn in his flesh. He begged God three times to take it away. God responded to Paul saying that his grace was sufficient and that his power would be made perfect in Paul's weakness. This passage showed me that God uses our 'weaknesses' to demonstrate his power."[5]

As an intern with Joni and Friends' Cause 4 Life program, Kristin served as a short-term missionary in Uganda, helping children affected by disability. As her hope in Christ and her identify in Christ grew and deepened, she wanted to share that same hope with people who needed to know of the eternal reward ahead of them. "I have learned that I can use my brokenness to serve others because I see people here who are so broken and they're in need of hope," Kristin said.[6]

If you're counseling a child facing a terminal diagnosis or one who seems to be losing their battle with cancer or another potentially life-threatening disease, it is crucial to help them understand eternity. Assure them that it may not make sense on earth, but in heaven they'll completely understand God's good purposes in allowing suffering to touch their life.

Jeff Robinson, a father of four and a pastor, says the Bible doesn't shrink from the topic of death, and neither should we. He says death is a part of our fallen world, and he advises parents that specific verses like Psalm 139 can bring children comfort when explained in a way that is age-appropriate.[7]

There are also good children's books that deal with heaven, such as *Goodbye to Goodbyes* by Lauren Chandler (Tales That Tell the Truth, The Good Book Company, 2019) and *God Made Me for Heaven* by Marty Machowski (New Growth Press, coming Spring 2021). Another illustrated children's book that reassures children of God's love in the face of hard circumstances is *The Moon Is Always Round* by Jonathan Gibson (New Growth Press, 2019). As you read these books with children (or read them to them), use them as a starting point for letting them express their fears, doubts, and questions. As always, the resurrected Jesus is our firm foundation and anchor for our souls and the souls of the littlest ones.

A Word to Parents

There's a reason we have the expression, "mama bear." It's one thing to have pain or suffering inflicted on us, but it's an entirely different struggle to watch your child endure the effects of a debilitating disease.

On her radio program, Joni shared the story of one mother's honest and angry response to her daughter's terminal diagnosis:

> Gloria fell into a deep anguish when she learned how serious her daughter's illness was. Little Laura, it seemed, had already suffered enough from the degenerative nerve disease she'd been born with, but now, the doctors' forecast included more suffering and impending death. Like any mother, Gloria desperately wished that she could take away Laura's pain and discomfort. She vacillated from sullen times of sorrow to furious outbursts of anger.

And Gloria had no problem with the idea of God's sovereignty and his control of her daughter's illness. If God was sovereign she knew exactly who to blame! One night, she left her child's bedside and paused in the hallway, trying to quiet her anger and dry her tears. And she remembers whispering, "God, it's not right! It's not right! You've never had to watch one of your children die!"

At that point, Gloria clasped her hand over her mouth. The truth hit her. God most certainly did watch his child die—his one and only child. And like any parent, he probably wished he could have taken away his Son's pain. Yet God endured the pain because God so loved the world. Just like it says in John 3:16, "For God so loved the world that he gave his one and only Son, that whoever believes in him shall not perish but have eternal life." [NIV] Gloria's heavenly Father endured the pain of his Son's death so that she and her daughter could have life everlasting.

That fact alone buoyed up Gloria's demoralized spirit. She could bear the pain of her daughter's suffering and death because God bore the pain of his Son's suffering and death. It meant that God's strength and empathy were tailor-made for her. And he did not only die for her, he lives to give her power and strength to endure what seems to be the unendurable. He even lives to give her daughter that kind of hidden strength! Gloria could rest in the comfort that God was by her side in the most amazing parent support group ever devised! [8]

When our child is faced with a life-changing diagnosis, it can be tempting to turn away from God and doubt his goodness. Our suffering only makes sense if we understand both God's sovereignty and his sacrifice. Apart from a loving God, who uses suffering for his glory, our pain is meaningless. But in his hands, disease, disability, even death can become a means of bringing others to faith in Jesus Christ.

Although Joni has seen God do this in her own life and through the lives of those served by the ministry, she's learned that at first hurting people simply want us to "weep with those who weep" (Romans 12:15). Then, they'll likely be open to hearing from Scripture.

"God's got his reasons for allowing so much pain and heartache and suffering, and those reasons are good and right and true. But I will be the first to tell you that when your heart is being wrung out like a sponge, an orderly list of the sixteen good biblical reasons as to why this is happening, can sting like salt in the wound," Joni said. "You don't stop the bleeding with the answers. Oh yes, there comes a time when people stop asking 'Why?' with a clenched fist and start asking 'Why?' with a searching heart. And that's a great time for the Bible's answers. But when the suffering is fresh, answers don't always reach the problem where it hurts, and that's in the gut and in the heart."[9]

Pastor and author Costi Hinn agrees that hurting parents need to take time to process their anger and disappointment and let go of what they thought life would look like. Then, we must encourage them to bring it all back to lay at the foot of the cross.

"Your anxieties and pain belong at his feet (1 Peter 5:7), and he promises peace beyond human comprehension to those who come to him with prayerful, thankful, dependent hearts (Philippians 4:6–7)," Costi said, sharing his own family's

struggles after their three-month-old son, Timothy, was diagnosed with cancer. "God grows us, shapes us, sanctifies us,
and brings us to the end of ourselves through suffering. All
the while molding us into the image of His Son Jesus. This
doesn't mean that we should be excited about a cancer diagnosis, or hoping our child suffers. But it does mean that we
should not be so obsessed with our relief that we miss out on
the lessons God teaches us along the way. Suffering brings us
closer to God, and through suffering He accomplishes great
purposes."[10]

God wants to use our struggles to remind us of our dependence on him and on each other. If you're in a season of
isolation, be intentional about finding a safe and supportive
community of believers. If your life seems to consist of running from one doctor's appointment to the next or your child
is in need of constant care, your supportive community may
need to start online. Either way, don't fail to find other parents
who can empathize with your pain and come alongside you.

Amy Mason wrote her book, *Bible Promises for Parents of
Children with Special Needs*, for hurting parents searching for
answers. "In times of great loss, you may be tempted to give
up on God. You may doubt him and wonder why he didn't
prevent this loss. The Bible tells you that troubles will come—
things will be lost and your feelings will be hurt. Yet the Bible
also encourages you not to throw out your confident hope.
When you are grieving and fear the emptiness ahead, seek
refuge in the presence of God. He is a God who rewards those
who trust him when it hurts and cling to him when they have
nothing else. You have this hope: God loves to redeem great
loss for abundant blessing."[11]

CHAPTER 15
COUNSELING CHILDREN WITH A DISABILITY
JONI AND FRIENDS

The room was quiet as eyes darted back and forth between tests and answer sheets, with No. 2 pencils hard at work. Looking around the classroom, Matthew started to tap, tap, tap his pencil.

"Shhh!" someone hissed from across the room.

He tried to sit still, he really did, but Matthew was not good at being still or quiet. He knew he was trying his teacher's patience. He knew his parents were tired of getting notes from school. He rubbed his thumb back and forth along the rubber therapy tool hidden just inside his desk. Sometimes it helped. But other times it didn't, and Matthew found himself getting angry—a lot.

With his desk sitting near Mrs. Henderson, he overheard the test administrator's whispers. "He just filled in the circles," the man said in hushed tones. "This test is supposed to take an hour—there's no way he did it in under fifteen minutes."

"I understand," Mrs. Henderson responded, "but he loves math. Can you please just check his work to make sure?"

The man grumbled something as he asked Matthew to hand him his answer sheet covered in shaded circles. He went to the back of the room and after a few minutes returned to let Mrs. Henderson know that Matthew scored 98 percent. She looked at Matthew with a big smile and then put her finger to her lips, reminding him that the other students still needed quiet.

That day was a small victory in a long line of disappointments—something many children with disabilities and their parents can relate to. Matthew's autism diagnosis as a toddler helped his parents understand his social challenges, but it didn't help him make friends or ease the tension and isolation he experienced at school.

According to Autism Speaks, an advocacy and research organization, "Autism spectrum disorder (ASD), refers to a broad range of conditions characterized by challenges with social skills, repetitive behaviors, speech and nonverbal communication."[1] Statistics from the Centers for Disease Control and Prevention estimate that 1 in 59 children in the United States will be diagnosed with some form of autism.

Dr. Mark Shaw says *spectrum* is appropriate because each person with autism is unique, with a range of strengths and weaknesses. "Having counseled, befriended, and loved people described as autistic, it is helpful to me to think of this spectrum with two extreme points and all sorts of in between levels of behaviors and thinking. I have seen the spectrum depicted as both linear and circular."[2]

One end of the spectrum includes individuals who are considered "severely challenged," while on the other end are those who are described as "highly skilled." Most counselors working with those who have an autism diagnosis will be dealing with children like Matthew who function at a higher level.

"Aren't we glad that the Bible teaches the eternal worth and dignity of all humans regardless of their function or contributions to society?" Dr. Shaw shared in a blog for the Biblical Counseling Coalition. "Being made in the image of God gives every human being value and purpose regardless of what is considered typical or nontypical functioning."[3]

Sadly, there is much less empathy or understanding for those who live with what are sometimes referred to as "hidden disabilities." There are many learning disabilities, emotional disorders, and some physical disabilities that may not be obvious: early multiple sclerosis, chronic fatigue syndrome, debilitating food sensitivities, seizures, and others.

Kathy Kuhl, an author and mother of a grown son with attention deficit disorder, ended up homeschooling her son and then became a voice of support for families that often face unfair judgment due to a disability. She wants to increase awareness of the struggles for children and their parents when a family is impacted by disability. She wrote in an unpublished resource for Joni and Friends,

> These children and teens with hidden disabilities don't look any different. They walk and run, and some may be gifted athletes, but they face tremendous invisible challenges.
>
> For parents of children with these invisible disorders, the stresses are different than for other parents. Being misunderstood hurts. A mother told me that once, at the playground, she watched another boy snatch something from her son, who has multiple disabilities. Her son exploded, hitting and screaming. She wanted to correct her child, but she knew he was too upset to listen. Over time she learned a firm hug is what he needed to calm him down so he could listen. She also knew that to every parent on the playground it looked like she was rewarding aggression with sympathy. We face pressure from friends, neighbors, and relatives. Some of them believe that if we'd just discipline our kids better, they wouldn't be so forgetful, impulsive, upset, or socially awkward. Or they tell the child, "You just need to try harder."

Shaw Bates was diagnosed with a learning disorder as a child and knows it's not about a lack of effort. "When I learn, it's like climbing a ladder, but for people who learn normally, they can take the escalators," Shaw said. For students with learning disorders such as dyslexia (reading), dyscalculia (math), and dysgraphia (writing), their brains receive and process information differently and can require individual learning strategies. Both doctors and teachers told Shaw and his parents that he could not learn.

Although he looked like any other ten-year-old boy, Shaw's disability left him feeling isolated and alone in his struggles through much of his childhood. "I was with kids who had physical disabilities and some with severe mental disorders. I was often called 'stupid' and 'retarded.' I did not have any friends," he shared.

Shaw eventually discovered how he could learn best and with some support systems went on to graduate from Biola University. While serving as an intern with Joni and Friends, he provided insights into the struggles of children with hidden disabilities. "The feelings I had were that I was stupid, slow, and not good at anything," Shaw said. "I would cry out to God, *Why am I stupid? Why am I not smart? And why do I have a learning disability?*"[4]

Nick Vujicic was born with no arms and no legs, but he defied any limitations people tried to place on him because of his physical disability. He is a husband, father, author, and an evangelist who travels the world inspiring others through the international nonprofit ministry he founded. His father, Boris, says that although Nick experienced struggles early on, the family kept pointing Nick back to God and what he *could* do.

"We always fought any attempt to label or marginalize Nick because we wanted our bright and unstoppable son to have every opportunity to prove his value in the world," Boris said. "Subjective assessments, perceptions, and prejudices are illusory. All children have strengths and weaknesses, and they can surprise you in so many ways. Our duty is to nurture, encourage, and motivate them, and help them build upon their strengths."[5]

No Easy Answers

As a counselor you may be meeting with children like Matthew or Shaw with hidden disabilities, or you may be asked to counsel a child with physical limitations like Nick. As we serve families affected by disability at Joni and Friends, we find "why questions" are a common thread for both children and parents.

Why would God let this happen?
Why do I struggle with _____ and my friends don't?
Why can't people see that I'm trying?
Why can't people look beyond my limitations?

While we don't have all the answers, we can trust that God's Word will bring comfort, and we don't shy away from honest questions. Joni Eareckson Tada has been a quadriplegic for more than fifty years as a result of a diving accident at seventeen. After wrestling with her own depression and anger, she eventually founded Joni and Friends to not only be a voice for those impacted by disability and help churches come alongside them but also to provide a safe place for hurting people to find encouragement from God's Word.

When it comes to the "Why?" question, we are more like the child who, when he painfully scrapes his knee, doesn't want Daddy to lecture him on "why you fell off your bike"; rather, the child just wants Daddy to pick him up, pat him on the back, and tell him everything is going to be okay: "Daddy's here, honey, it's okay." And that's our unspoken cry to our Heavenly Father. When we are hurting and confused, we want Fatherly assurance that our world is not splitting apart at the seams. What's more, we want our Father to be in the center of our suffering, bearing and sharing our load. And that's what the God of the Bible does. He's not quick to give us answers, but he is quick to give himself.[6]

As a counselor, your goal is to help families affected by disability understand that all persons, with or without disabilities, are created in God's image, according to Genesis 1:26–27. Lilly Park, former assistant professor of biblical counseling at The Southern Baptist Theological Seminary, writing in a blog for the Biblical Counseling Coalition, says, "Fundamentally, it means that we are not defined by our disabilities and are not incomplete because of a disability."[7]

Children need to understand that although we live in a broken world due to sin, God has a purpose for every one of us—regardless of our abilities. Moses lacked confidence and didn't believe he could be used by God due to a speech impediment. You can share with a child Exodus 4:11 where this is addressed:

Then the LORD asked Moses, "Who makes a person's mouth? Who decides whether people speak or do not speak, hear or do not hear, see or do not see? Is it not I, the LORD? (NLT)

Remind children that God has a unique plan for each of us and that the Bible teaches that we are woven together in our mothers' bodies with special care.

You made all the delicate, inner parts of my body
and knit me together in my mother's womb.
(Psalm 139:13 NLT)

You might find it helpful to use embroidery or a tapestry to help explain this concept. Some children might relish an opportunity for active learning, as you help them create a small embroidery project available at craft stores. The point is to show them that when we look at life's problems from the bottom "messy" side, they don't make sense at all. But when we view the tapestry or embroidery from the top side, we see that all the different stitched threads make a beautiful design. Until we get to heaven, we cannot see the complete picture and God's purpose for our struggles, but we can continue to trust that he created us with care.

What Did Jesus Do?

Often, children affected by disability experience social isolation and struggle with wanting to belong. You can introduce them to their friend Jesus. He will never look down on them and will always be with them. He always hears them when they cry. He wants them to tell him all about whatever is troubling them. Throughout Scripture, Jesus was caring and compassionate to those with disabilities, healing them and restoring them to community whenever possible.

God designed Christians to do life together, so it's painful when we are excluded or ostracized, especially when it's due to something beyond our control, such as a disability. The apostle Paul compared believers to the parts of a body that need each other to function properly. Share 1 Corinthians 12:20–23 to show God's plan for inclusion:

> Yes, there are many parts, but only one body. The eye can never say to the hand, "I don't need you." The head can't say to the feet, "I don't need you."
>
> In fact, some parts of the body that seem weakest and least important are actually the most necessary. And the parts we regard as less honorable are those we clothe with the greatest care. (NIV)

Children need to understand that in Jesus's time those with disabilities were excluded because many people thought they had done something wrong and their disability was a punishment or a curse. You might take a minute to address this issue specifically and ask whether he or she has ever had similar thoughts. Read John 9:1–7 where Jesus healed a man who had been blind since birth. He told his disciples that the man's disability was not because of anything he'd done, but it was part of God's plan to help others see God's power and goodness in difficult circumstances.

A Word to Parents

Jesus revealed God's power, but he also displayed his tenderness. He understands your every pain and sorrow and the brokenness we live with, especially when our families have been impacted by disability. He hears the desperate pleas of a mother, crying out to know *what* she can do to help her child's loneliness, or a father grappling with *how* to let go of the dreams he had for his child, so he can embrace a different dream.

We can bring our hurts to the foot of the cross, but we should also find caring, supportive believers to come alongside us. In 2 Corinthians 1:3–4 we read that God is the source of all comfort, but then he wants to use us to comfort others: "When they are troubled, we will be able to give them the same comfort God has given us." (NLT)

Kathy Kuhl has seen God redeem her son's struggles and her own expanded knowledge of parenting and homeschooling to change the trajectory of their lives. She now helps other parents as she writes and speaks throughout the country.

"There were days I wept," Kathy said. "We don't need to pretend to be happy all the time. Jesus wept too. He is the Man of Sorrows, acquainted with grief. We can have good reasons to weep:

- We weep for our kids. This is a broken world. That brokenness hurts most when it touches those we love. We weep for their pain. I've grieved because learning was so hard for my son. We weep for our children when other kids are cruel. I've grieved with friends whose daughters battled mental illness.
- We weep for the death of our dreams. That's okay too. When we give up the life we imagined, God doesn't require us to do that stoically, as if it costs us nothing.
- Sometimes, we cry with a new diagnosis. While a diagnosis can be a relief, it can also bring a flood of new questions, worries, specialists, treatments, and

medications. Sometimes our children receive different diagnoses as they grow, and the news can hurt. Suddenly, we have a new set of specialists, terms, therapies, and acronyms to master, a new prognosis to come to terms with, or question.

- We cry because we are sick of uncertainty and instability. It can be hard, even impossible to understand what causes our children's difficulties. Parents of children with multiple sclerosis and other physical disorders never know what their kids will be able to do that day.

When the weeping has ended, we can once again turn to Scripture to find our source of hope—Jesus.

> We are pressed on every side by troubles, but we are not crushed. We are perplexed, but not driven to despair. We are hunted down, but never abandoned by God. We get knocked down, but we are not destroyed. Through suffering, our bodies continue to share in the death of Jesus so that the life of Jesus may also be seen in our bodies. (2 Corinthians 4:8–10 NLT)

Amy Mason who wrote the encouraging book, *Bible Promises for Parents of Children with Special Needs*,[8] shares that, "When you've just received a hard diagnosis or realized that dream of yours won't come true, you may feel hopeless, like you're drowning in emotional pain or stumbling around in darkness. But you are not lost to God. He knows what you long for, and he knows your needs as well as your child's. He wants to be a part of the process of creating new dreams with you. Cry out to him and share your heart. Ask him to give you a new dream for you and your family. Hope gives you the strength to endure many hard circumstances."

As a quadriplegic person who's fought cancer twice and lives with chronic pain, Joni knows that suffering and disability can force us to examine what we really believe.

> We hate it when life isn't fair! We expect our families to have the good life, with long stretches of ease and comfort and only occasional interruptions or irritations—frustrating, but easily bearable. Nothing bursts that bubble more quickly than a disabilty. It reminds me of my friend Susan who, when she learned that the child she was carrying had multiple disabilities, collapsed into her husband's arms and sobbed, "Our lives will never be the same! Never!" Brad held Susan tight, stroking and kissing her hair. Then he whispered, "Sweetheart, maybe our lives aren't supposed to be the same."[9]

Reflecting back, Boris Vujicic advises new parents to let go of their expectations and what they think it will be like to raise their child with special needs and instead embrace God's plan.

"We came to see Nick as God's beautiful creation, lovingly formed in His image. We lacked the wisdom, initially, to understand that. We saw Nick as disabled rather than enabled. We could not grasp that his missing arms and legs were part of God's plan for our son," Boris said. "Nick gave us a new definition of the ideal child and a deeper appreciation for the complexity of our Father's divine vision."[10]

Children and Trauma

CHAPTER 16
HELPING ABUSED CHILDREN

AMY BAKER

Thirteen-year-old Ruby hates going to bed at night. She was eight years old when her mother's husband began sexually abusing her. She didn't know that prior to this he was trying to groom her for his abuse. She thought his gifts, attention, and sweet words were because he genuinely loved her. But that all changed when the sexual molestation started. Nighttime became dangerous. During the night, her stepfather would creep into her room and do unspeakable things. Even when her stepfather didn't come into her room, Ruby would lay awake wondering, *Why were you so nice to me today? Are you going to get me? Will someone find out what you are doing to me? How can I get away from you?* For Ruby, nighttime is a time to be vigilant, not a time to sleep.

Believing her stepfather's threats that if she told anyone the cops would take her away and she would never see her mom and little sister, Ruby kept silent for five years. She had learned that trying to protect herself by refusing her stepfather only resulted in more pain and punishment. Once when she refused to do what her stepfather demanded, he had taken the family dog that Ruby loved and shot it in front of her.

Ruby also tried to protect herself in other ways. She tried to keep as hidden and unnoticed as she could when her stepfather was home. But sleeping on the floor in a corner of her room hadn't prevented her stepdad from finding her. She tried to make herself physically unattractive, but her ratty, smelly clothes and unkempt appearance had resulted in ridicule, not safety.

Over the years, Ruby became more and more isolated. She felt that getting close to someone posed risk—the risk that her story would come out and more abuse would follow. Her stepfather took precautions to prevent her from building relationships outside the house, but even without his controlling restrictions, Ruby didn't feel she had anything to contribute to relationships. What did she say to the girls talking about their first kiss when she had already had sex with her stepdad?

Lying has become easy. Ruby has learned to lie about her abuse so that her stepfather won't hurt her or something she loves. Ruby has learned to lie to family and friends so they won't find out how dirty and unlovable she is. But lying has led to deep regret now that her little sister has been abused. *If only, if only, if only*, she thinks, *then my sister wouldn't have been abused.*

When she learned that her stepfather had started abusing her little sister, Ruby finally confided in a teacher at school. Now that the abuse has been brought to light, Ruby has new fears that haunt her—fears that her stepfather will come back to harm her (although he is currently in jail); fears that people won't believe her story; fears that her mom will be arrested for not stopping her stepdad; fears that everyone will know what happened and look at her as if she's some kind of freak.

All these terrors come out in nightmares when she tries to sleep. Ruby hates going to bed at night.

Where Do You Start?

As a vulnerable child, Ruby has been treated as an object to satisfy someone else's wicked desires. The powerful domination of her abuser to ensure that he could make her do what he wanted has left her with fear, anxiety, shame, pain, alienation, and anger. Because her abuser groomed her for his abuse by telling her she was beautiful, smart, fun, etc., Ruby never trusts anyone who praises her. Being treated nicely and praised means her body will become an object to be touched, sneered at, and broken to the will of an abuser. You'll often find these responses present in children who have been abused.

Not surprisingly, fear and anxiety often plague victims of abuse. These precious victims have been taught to fear the abuser's cruel use of his or her power over them. This applies not only to the abuse itself but also to the threats and bribes that usually accompany the abuse. For many, fear and anxiety become their unwanted, constant companions. They may try out defensive maneuvers like withdrawing from social contact, sleeping fully clothed or with several layers of clothes, mentally going to a different place while their bodies are being violated, running away, or turning to drugs or alcohol to get relief. While at some level they realize these are ineffective ways of achieving protection and peace, they feel compelled to continue these strategies because they believe that if they let go, all that would remain is utter terror.

While anger is an appropriate response to wickedness, sometimes anger is just a cover-up for fear. When this is the case, anger is misdirected and used to keep others away, including those who have not treated the child wickedly. As one girl said, being angry was easier than being scared. And being angry can feel empowering. Fear and hurt can be masked or squelched by this other emotion. So anger may be the mask that covers up deeper hurts—being devalued, rejected, powerless, unlovable, unimportant, shamed, and abused. As a counselor, you may find that you first need to address issues like fear, shame, and rejection before you address anger toward you and others who were not the abuser.

Of course, not all abused children display anger. Responses to abuse are not formulaic. As in all counseling, we need to thoughtfully and carefully work toward understanding the heart.

Realize Trust Has Been Broken

As you begin to counsel an abused child, keep in mind that he or she will probably find it difficult to trust you. In some ways, this is an appropriate and righteous position. The Lord says, "Cursed is the man [person] who trusts in man" (Jeremiah 17:5). An abused child has learned through difficult experience not to trust at least one adult. Of course, every biblical counselor, no matter how wise or godly, fails to fully and perfectly represent the One true and righteous God. So while we are called to be trustworthy, we must never lead children to believe that we are intrinsically worthy of their confidence.

However, as biblical counselors, we are given the opportunity to reveal to the child the trustworthiness of the Hero of the Universe. The one truly trustworthy person is the God and man Jesus who was willing to endure terrifying abuse himself to rescue us from the dominion of this dark world and throw open the door to heaven.

Trusting Jesus will likely not blossom based upon a simple introduction. It develops through moving from acquaintanceship to intimacy, from being casually familiar to having a relationship of love. Developing trust is a process that takes time, so give the children an opportunity to process this in their developing relationship with God.

Those who have been abused are often left with a conviction that God does not care for them. They may be surprised to learn that people in the Bible thought the same thing. Lamentations 3 describes in awful detail the cry of Jeremiah, who was abused by the people of his homeland. Jeremiah asserts that even when he calls out or cries for help, God has shut out his prayer (v. 8).

Jeremiah is not the only one who is convinced he has been forsaken by God. The psalmist in Psalm 22 says that he cries out day and night, but God doesn't answer. On the cross, God's own Son echoes this despair as he cries out in a loud voice "My God, my God, why have you forsaken me?" (Matthew 27:46).

Yet each conviction of abandonment is turned on its head. There is much more that happens in each of these stories. Jeremiah declares,

> The LORD is good to those whose hope is in him,
>   to the one who seeks him;
> it is good to wait quietly
>   for the salvation of the LORD.
> For no one is cast off
>   by the Lord forever.
> Though he brings grief, he will show compassion,
>   so great is his unfailing love.

For he does not willingly bring affliction
   or grief to anyone.
   (Lamentations 3:25, 26, 31, 32, 33 NIV)

The psalmist declares:

He has not despised or scorned
   the suffering of the afflicted one;
he has not hidden his face from him
   but has listened to his cry for help.
   (Psalm 22:24 NIV)

And God raised his beloved Son Jesus from the dead (Matthew 28). He was *not* forsaken by his Father. God is trustworthy, powerful, and compassionate. God never abandons those who belong to him.

Unveil Our Trustworthy God

There are many passages you can use as examples that when God says something, it happens. God says about himself in Isaiah 49:23, "those who hope in me *will not* be disappointed" (NIV, emphasis added).

You could take the child through a number of passages, asking her to identify what God says, and then what happens. The following verses provide examples (of course, there are many, many other passages you could use):

- Genesis 1:3 (NIV)—And God said, "Let there be light," and there was light.
  - » What did God say? [Let there be light.]

» What happened when God said this? [There was light.]
» When God says something, it happens.

- John 5:8–9 (NIV)—Then Jesus said to him, "Get up! Pick up your mat and walk." At once the man was cured; he picked up his mat and walked.
  » What did Jesus say? [Get up, pick up your mat and walk.]
  » What happened? [The man was cured, he picked up his mat and walked.]
  » When God says something, it happens.

- John 11:43–44 (NIV)—Jesus called in a loud voice, "Lazarus, come out!" The dead man came out, his hands and feet wrapped with strips of linen, and a cloth around his face.
  » What did Jesus say to the dead man? [Come out.]
  » What happened? [Lazarus came to life and came out.]
  » When God says something, it happens.

To the abused child you are counseling this may seem hard to believe. Gently and slowly review the truth with her and give her time to absorb it. There is nothing wrong with going over the same truth repeatedly as you give the Spirit of God the opportunity to impact her heart. God has good plans for her. His heart toward her is the same heart that is shown in Jeremiah 29:11 in speaking to Israel.

"For I know the plans I have for you," declares the LORD, "plans to prosper you and not to harm you, plans to give you hope and a future" (NIV).

God lifts the poor and needy from the garbage pile (Psalm 113:7); he heals the brokenhearted and binds up their wounds (Psalm 147:3). Ruby's abuser has treated her like garbage—an object to be used, crumpled up, and tossed into the trash when no longer needed. But God picks people up out of the garbage bin where they have been discarded by others, and he places them with princes (Psalm 113:8).

God's heart toward children who have been abused is to make them royalty, daughters and sons of the King. God wants to give them a crown of beauty instead of ashes, joy instead of mourning, and praise instead of despair. As they grow in trust, they can radiate the very splendor of God (Isaiah 61:3).

Anticipate a Desire for Power and Control

If you were Ruby, lying awake in a corner of your room at night, wondering whether your stepfather was going to come after you, wouldn't you long for power and control? If you were Ruby, haunted with questions—*Are you going to be home? Are you going to get me? How can I get away from you?*—wouldn't you long for power and control? If you were Ruby, filled with guilt and grief because you've just learned your stepfather has begun abusing your little sister, wouldn't you long for power and control? Often those who have been abused as children go through life looking for power and control, either in themselves or in someone else.

Children who have been abused need a protector. They need power. God can supply both!

Those who have been abused are often desperately aware of their powerlessness. This is exactly how the righteous King Jehoshaphat felt in 2 Chronicles 20:12.

Our God, will you not judge them? For we have no power to face this vast army that is attacking us. We do not know what to do, but our eyes are on you. (NIV)

King Jehoshaphat saw that he was powerless, but he also saw something else. He saw the Lord was mighty.

"O LORD, God of our fathers, are you not God in heaven? You rule over all the kingdoms of the nations. In your hand are power and might, so that none is able to withstand you. (2 Chronicles 20:6)

We want to help Ruby, her little sister, and others like her see that they can depend on the power of the Lord. He is their protector, and he works righteousness and justice for all the oppressed (see Colossians 1:9–13; Ephesians 3:14–19).

Christ died for the powerless, and it's his desire to save us, to rescue us from the dominion of darkness, and to strengthen us with *all power* according to **his** glorious might (Romans 5:6).

As a counselor, your words alone will not convince Ruby that God has all power and control and can rescue her. But you can talk to God on her behalf as you meet together. You can pray with and for Ruby, much like Paul prayed for those he loved in Ephesians 3:14–19 and Colossians 1: 9–13.

Ruby, since the day we heard about you, we have not stopped praying for you and asking God to strengthen you with power in your inner being. Ruby, we pray this in order that you may live a life worthy of the Lord and may please him in every way: bearing fruit in every good work, growing in the knowledge of God, *being strengthened with **all power** according to his glorious might **so that*** you may have great endurance and patience. Ruby, we pray that you may have power to grasp how wide and long and high and deep is the love of Christ. (Author paraphrase)

Our Protector rescues us and give us **all** power. Why? What should we do with that power?

Use power to endure. (Colossians 1:11)

The effects of abuse often seem unendurable, but God's power allows us to have great endurance. For these precious children who have been abused, it often seems as if the pain of the abuse will never end—that it will haunt them for the rest of their lives. It is true that their victimization can't be erased, but with God's power they can endure and not be locked into an identity as a victim. God strengthens us with all power so that we can endure.

Use power to grow in the knowledge of God and to learn to trust biblically. (Colossians 1:10)

Remember that abused children often find it difficult to trust anyone. Or, when they do begin to trust, they put all their confidence in the object of their trust and expect that person to never let them down.

Why does this happen? Because these scared, abused children are functioning according to their own understanding. What they understand is that they have been hurt and they don't want to be hurt again. Paradoxically, however, God tells us to lean not on our own understanding.

Trust in the LORD with all your heart and lean not on your
own understanding; in all your ways submit to him, and
he will make your paths straight. (Proverbs 3:5–6 NIV)

It can seem almost impossible to give up trusting in oneself. It feels dangerous and vulnerable. But, as they take step by
faltering step to grow in the knowledge of God and he gives
the power to grasp how wide and long and high and deep his
love is, these children can move from trusting in themselves to
trusting in the Lord. Psalm 9 assures us this is true: "Those who
know your name will trust in you, for you, LORD, have never
forsaken those who seek you" (v. 10 NIV). Jeremiah 17 adds,
"But blessed is the one who trusts in the LORD, whose confidence is in him. They will be like a tree planted by the water
that sends out its roots by the stream. It does not fear when heat
comes; its leaves are always green. It has no worries in a year of
drought and never fails to bear fruit" (vv. 7–8 NIV).

As you work through this, you might ask the child to give
you some examples of how they have trusted in themselves
and it didn't turn out well. For example, the child might have
lied about studying for a math test but then failed the test and
got assigned extra problems to complete. Or, the child may
have gotten mad and told her best friend she hated her but
felt really bad after she said it. Additionally, you can ask the
child what it would look like in her life if she were to take a
step toward trusting God and not herself. For a fearful child,
perhaps a step of trust would be saying hello when greeted by
an adult while she is with her parent. Perhaps a step of trust
would be to cooperate honestly with authorities whom God
has designated to investigate and prosecute her abuser. Pray

with the child, asking God to strengthen him or her with all power so that he or she can take a step of trust.

These are only some of the beginning steps of the counseling process. Expect that just as the child may have been abused for a long time, working through what has happened may also take a long time. You may also find that you will meet with a child for a number of months, get to a good place, and then get involved again as new questions and issues come to the surface. Don't expect that everything will be resolved in one round of counseling; be available to help over the long haul as needed.

A Word to Parents

Discovering that your child has been abused is likely one of the hardest things you will ever face in this life. You may be struggling with the same emotions you see your child struggling with, and you may be wondering how you can possibly help your child when you feel desperate yourself.

Cry out to God. He is a Father who understands the deep hurt of seeing his child cruelly abused. He can sympathize.

Not only can he sympathize, he has the power to help. Begin to keep a journal of your laments. But also include the ways you have already seen God helping, comforting, and healing. The Lord is close to the brokenhearted, and he binds up their wounds. Even now, he is tenderly binding your wounds. Knowing Jesus brings a sweetness that will always be stronger than the most bitter of circumstances on earth.[1]

Pray with your child as others before you have prayed, pouring out their hearts before the Lord and pleading with him for the strength to trust and turn to him. Talk to your child about ways you see him answering your prayers.

I'm certain this chapter has not addressed many areas where you want help. A number of other chapters in this book offer guidance so I would encourage you to read them even though they are not specifically written about abuse. For example, you will probably appreciate Julie Lowe's chapter on anxiety, Edward Welch's chapter on shame, and Michael Emlet's chapter on anger as you continue on this path with your child.

Don't endure this in isolation from others. God wants his people to mourn with those who mourn, and he knows you need others. He wants to use your brothers and sisters in Christ to help comfort you in your sorrow. While being around others may seem difficult right now, and you hate that others see you crying, please don't withdraw. You need your brothers and sisters in Christ, and your child needs them as well.

You may also find it helpful to seek out biblical counseling for yourself as well as for your child. You may find that your struggles are very similar to those of your child and that it's hard to know what to say and do when you're wrestling with similar issues. Or you might find that your struggles look different than those of your child and you're having trouble relating to how your child is processing what has happened to him or her. Having the help of a wise biblical counselor can encourage you as you navigate these difficult waters.

Be prepared for your child to wrestle in different ways as he or she gets older. While a child may initially struggle with fear or anger, you may find that at the time of puberty new questions and struggles come into play. Questions about body image and identity may become more important than they were originally. Then, as your child reaches marriageable age, a new set of questions may arise: Will anyone want me? What will sex in marriage be like? Am I damaged goods?

As deep and as painful as your suffering is currently, it is not God's plan for it to remain that way forever. A time is coming when God will wipe away every tear from the eyes of those who belong to him. God himself will come to dwell with us and there will be no more mourning, no more crying, and no more pain (Revelation 21:3–4). The waiting period may include tears, but even in the midst of sorrow God is at work refining your faith and making you strong, firm, and steadfast (1 Peter 5:10; 2 Peter 1:7). Continue to trust in him and cling to his Word.

CHAPTER 17
COUNSELING CHILDREN OF DIVORCE

AMY BAKER

Ten-year-old Marianna lives with Mom Tuesdays through Thursdays and every other weekend, and with Dad on Mondays and every other weekend. Her parents have been legally divorced for six months, but the process began two years ago when Dad moved out of their home to live with another woman. Before this, Marianna had been happy-go-lucky, frequently seen skipping beside her mom with a Disney princess doll in her arms. At eight years old, Marianna had been an average student, made friends easily, and loved everything princess.

Marianna found out her parents were divorcing on Christmas Day, though that wasn't the original plan. Initially, her parents planned to celebrate the holidays as a family and wait until the new year to tell Marianna and separate. However, when Dad stepped out of the room on Christmas morning to call his girlfriend while Marianna was opening her presents, her mom lost it. In the fierce argument that followed, Marianna learned that her dad was leaving her mom. He packed a bag and left that same day. Her mom shut herself in her bedroom and left Marianna wondering what to do with the Christmas present she had painstakingly made for her father. Today, at ten years old, Marianna will tell you that she hates Christmas.

At first Marianna thought that the divorce was her fault. She had heard her parents fighting about money and thought that maybe if she hadn't whined about wanting a new pair of shoes or a Disney princess bedroom, her parents wouldn't have been unhappy.

Marianna was also confused about how to relate to her parents. She felt sorry for her mom because her dad had left her, but she had often seen her mom be mean to her dad, so she didn't know what to think. Should she be loyal to her mom? To her dad? And how should she view her dad's girlfriend?

At times, Marianna has wished she could live by herself and never see either parent again. Sometimes she has shut herself up in her room to try to escape. When she can't escape the confusion and tension she feels, she gets angry. For example, one day when she was alone in her dad's apartment with his girlfriend, Marianna got into a fight with her about eating her lunch. When Marianna wouldn't eat the food on her plate, the girlfriend got angry and complained about Marianna upon her dad's return from an errand. Infuriated, Marianna hotly asked why she should have to obey someone who broke up their family.

Marianna had to change schools after the divorce. Her mom couldn't afford to stay in their home, and when they downsized, the new house was in a different school district. Marianna hasn't tried to make friends at her new school. It's easier to keep to herself than to explain to a new friend that her dad left her mom so she now lives with each parent part-time.

Unlike some children of divorce, Marianna's grades have improved. Because she has concluded that people you depend on can hurt you, Marianna intends to make good grades, get a degree in a field where she can make lots of money, and never depend on anyone again.

At this point, Marianna doesn't have much trust or respect for either parent. Because her mom seems to be hurting the most, Marianna has chosen to be loyal to her, but it's a loyalty that stems from duty, not love. She fights with both parents, and her parents fight with each other.

Going back and forth between her parents' homes has left Marianna feeling like a visitor in both places. When asked to describe herself, Marianna says, "I'm just a suitcase."

Being a Child of Divorce Is Hard and All Too Common

With the high rate of divorce in our culture, many of the children you counsel will have divorce in their family history, and it may not be something they experience just once. Most men and women who divorce go on to remarry and, sadly, the divorce rate is even higher for second marriages. This means that their children may live lives full of turmoil, with stepparents and stepsiblings coming in and out of their lives.

Not surprisingly, research shows that after a divorce, it's normal for children to struggle with the following responses:

1. Sadness and depression, fatigue, daydreams, spontaneous tears, withdrawal from friends, ineffective concentration, and, occasionally, focus on schoolwork as a means of withdrawing
2. Denial of what is happening
3. Embarrassment, which may last for years
4. Intense anger
5. Guilt over conflicting loyalties
6. Concern about being cared for, even if the family is affluent

7. Regression, lack of normal development, or return to dependency

8. Maturity foisted upon them by circumstances, which can separate them from peers

9. Physical symptoms, typically stomachaches or headaches[1]

In short, the children you counsel may face many struggles and temptations as a result of their parents' divorce.

Dealing with Conflicts in Loyalty

One of the most difficult things children face after their parents' divorce is the pressure they feel to choose sides. A nine-year-old girl I'll call Sophie said this:

> On Mother's Day I didn't know what to do. I didn't even know what I should do or could do. If I went with my stepmother, my mother would be furious. If I went with my mother, my stepmother would be upset. I couldn't even think about it. It's the worst situation I ever had in my life.[2]

Marianna also has ongoing loyalty conflicts. Recently her teacher announced that the class was having a special program and every student should invite their parents. When Marianna asked her dad, he said he wouldn't come unless he could bring his girlfriend. When she asked her mom, her mom said she wouldn't come if Dad's girlfriend came with him.

Mixed with the stress, confusion, and guilt from feeling as though they must choose sides is the fear of being abandoned by one or both parents. Both Sophie and Marianna face abandonment, at least temporarily, no matter what choice they make. If they choose Dad's side (or the side of their step-mother), their mother will, at least temporarily, withdraw love and treat them to some degree as an enemy. The reverse is also true. If they choose their mother, they risk rejection by their father (and stepmother).

When you're a child, how could you know if the abandonment will be temporary or permanent? You've just witnessed your parents permanently abandon each other. Will they abandon you as well? Even if a child has come to hate or despise one of his or her parents, no one wants to be hated back. We want people to feel bad when we hate them, not hate us in return. It's no wonder children describe this as the worst situation they have ever faced.

The gospel can become especially sweet in moments like these, because for those who trust in the Lord, even if their father and mother abandons them, the Lord never will. These dear children need to be able to cling to a Father who will never forsake them.

While there are many important passages you'll want to share with the children you counsel, let's look at the way one psalm shows children the love and help of the Lord. Psalm 27 provides a gospel opportunity and sweet comfort for children struggling with loyalty conflicts. Here are some suggestions on how to apply its truths to the children you counsel.

In Psalm 27:10 we hear the psalmist say,

> Even if my father and mother abandon me,
>   the Lord will hold me close. (NLT)

How precious is that! Even if the worst happens and my parents forsake me, God won't.

What gave the psalmist confidence that he wouldn't be abandoned by the Lord? Was it because he was such a good kid? Was it because he was smart, or funny, or a good athlete? No. He had confidence because the Lord had promised to be his salvation if he trusted in him. The psalmist makes it obvious throughout the psalm that this promise is the basis for his confidence. In verse 1, he declares, "The LORD is my light and my *salvation*" (emphasis added). In verse 9, he again identifies God as his *Savior*, his *salvation*. In other verses, he emphasizes that he trusts in the Lord because he seeks him and has confidence in him (vv. 4, 5, 8, 13).

Because God is his Savior, the psalmist is able to say, "Even if my mom and dad abandon me, the Lord will still want me." This is not wishful daydreaming on his part; this is a promise made by the Father himself to those who belong to him. God has said, "I will never leave you nor forsake you" (Hebrews 13:5). Remind children that when we come to God through Christ Jesus our Lord, we become *God's* children and nothing can separate us from his love (Romans 8:38–39). He will *never* abandon us.

Their situation can be tremendously difficult, but children who have the Lord as their Savior can receive great comfort from knowing that they will never be abandoned by him. As homework you might ask them to write out Psalm 27:10 and Romans 8:38–39 on a piece of art paper and decorate it to hang in their room. You might ask them to draw a picture of what these verses look like. You may encourage them to review these verses so often that they memorize them.

In future meetings, you might spend more time unpacking Psalm 27. Some points you may want the children to glean could include the following:

When the Lord is my light and salvation, I can be less afraid (v. 1)

> The LORD is my light and my salvation—
>   so why should I be afraid?
> The LORD is my fortress, protecting me from danger,
>   so why should I tremble? (NLT)

Ask the children to tell you some things that are scary to them because of their parents' divorce. There are all kinds of good reasons to be afraid. But when the Lord is our light and salvation, we can be less afraid. We're not dependent on our parents to save us or protect us from permanent harm. We have the Lord as our adopted Father (Romans 8:15).

The psalmist is not brave (unafraid) because everything in his life is good (vv. 2, 3, 5)

Point out that bad things are happening to this psalmist—people are attacking him. So the psalmist is not brave (unafraid) simply because everything in his life is safe and good. Yet, instead of being afraid, he will be confident. Why? Because of what he said in verse 1: God is his salvation and fortress. The psalmist continues in verse 5:

> For in the day of trouble
>   he will keep me safe in his dwelling;
> he will hide me in the shelter of his sacred tent
>   and set me high upon a rock. (NIV)

Explain to the child that when you belong to the Lord, God will protect you so that nothing that happens to you can do permanent damage to your soul. Nothing can hurt your soul beyond repair. In fact, God will use even the hard things for your good; he'll use them to make you more like Jesus (Romans 8:28–29).

The psalmist can be brave because the relationship he cares about most is with the Lord (v. 4)

The one thing I ask of the LORD—
    the thing I seek most—
is to live in the house of the LORD all the days of my life,
    delighting in the Lord's perfections
    and meditating in his Temple. (NLT)

You might ask the child to read verse 4 and tell you who the psalmist's BFF is. The psalmist's best friend forever is God. When God is your best friend forever, you can always (forever) turn to God, and he will be there to help you and love you.

Like the Psalmist, you can tell God you want his help (v. 7)

Hear, O LORD, when I cry with my voice,
    And be gracious to me and answer me. (NASB)

You can tell a child that when his or her parents divorce, it can seem like there is no one to help them. The child may try not to bother parents who are struggling. Or he or she may feel like they could get in trouble if they ask their parents for help. Remind the child that they can always ask God for help.

Like the psalmist, children don't need to worry that they're bothering God by asking for his help, or that he'll abandon them (remember v. 10). They are encouraged to ask God for his help. They don't need to act like they have to handle this struggle on their own.

Teach the child that God will often use his church to provide extra support. Sunday school teachers, children's or youth pastors, and friends' parents who know the Lord can reinforce them with God's help. Encourage the child to talk to these trusted adults about how they are struggling and to accept their help.

And you can decide to be loyal to God (v. 8)

It's really hard for a child to wrestle with whether they should be loyal to their mom or dad. Tell children in this situation that the psalmist had a loyalty decision to make too. He had to decide whether to be loyal to God or to someone else. According to this verse, he chose to be loyal to God.

> *When You said,* "Seek My face," my heart said to You,
> "Your face, O LORD, I shall seek." (NASB)

Explain that when God says, "Be loyal to me (seek my face)," we have a choice ("Your face, O LORD, I shall seek"). Being loyal to God means choosing to do what he says, as a child tries to love both parents. Being loyal to God means his opinion matters more than anyone else's. It means the child is always on *his* side.

You can guide the child to express something like this to the Lord: God, "I want to choose you first, not mom or dad. I want to be loyal to you because you love me and are loyally faithful to me." Explain that as they do this, they will begin to find that even when Mom and Dad are pressuring them to be loyal only to themselves, this won't have to be as upsetting as it used to be. Instead, the child can remember that God is with them and that he won't abandon them. The child is not as vulnerable as he or she would be if their mom or dad were their only source of security. Tell the child that God is their fortress, the one protecting them from any danger that would permanently destroy them, and that he will use all other danger to turn bad things into good for them through Jesus.

Agree with the child that it might be hard to tell their parents that they are going to work hard to love both parents well and that the only side they are going to choose is God's side. But reassure them that God will help them when they have to do hard things like this. Marianna can say to her parents, "Mom and Dad, I really want you to come to my special program at school. I know it's hard for the two of you to decide who should come and who shouldn't come. I want you both there and I will be hurt if one of you can't come. If you choose not to come, I'm sure I'll be sad during the program, but I'm going to ask God to help me remember that he is there and that he won't ever leave me. I'm going to ask God to help me do my best because I know that it's always safe to go to him."

Be confident that even if it's hard for a while, it won't always be this way (v. 13)

> Yet I am confident I will see the LORD's goodness
> while I am here in the land of the living. (NLT)

Help the child set their expectations realistically. Here is an example: "Sometimes, no matter what decision you make, someone will be mad. If you choose to go with your mom, your dad and stepmom may be upset. If you choose to go with your dad and stepmom, your mom may be angry.

"The psalmist also had people who were angry with him. Yet he was confident that he would get to see good things while he was alive. God tells us that now, for a little while, we may have to suffer grief in all kinds of hard things (1 Peter 1:6–7). But because of Jesus, the Father has something really good stored up for us (he calls it an inheritance), and this gift won't ever get taken away. We won't ever get tired of it, and we'll never find anything better. Until then, God promises to shield you with his power."

Wait for the Lord (v. 14)

> Wait patiently for the LORD.
>   Be brave and courageous.
>   Yes, wait patiently for the Lord. (NLT)

This is part of helping a child understand that their difficult situation won't go away right away. What is most important is to help them see that God can help the child to be strong, brave, and loyal to him. Like the psalmist, they can wait patiently for the Lord to make all things right (Isaiah 61:11) by trusting that God is good and does only good (Psalm 119:68). Tell them, "Remember, he won't forsake you, so even while you wait, he'll be with you. Talk to your pastor or Sunday school teacher about what you are experiencing. God wants to let them help you."

Dealing with Guilt

As a counselor, you may find that the children you counsel struggle with guilt. Like Marianna, they may believe they caused their parents' divorce. Even if their parents assure them the divorce is not their fault, children may find it difficult to trust that they are being told truth.

We've seen that children may also struggle with guilt due to loyalty conflicts. If they choose to be loyal to Mom, they may feel guilty because they didn't choose Dad, and vice versa. In such Catch-22 situations, children will suffer. Additionally, children may feel guilty for disobedient or hateful choices they have made.

You can help these dear children by taking time to talk about guilt so they can come to true and righteous conclusions. First, many children don't understand that guilt is fact first, not feeling first. We are guilty whenever we violate the standard for love and obedience to God that God has given us in his Word. You might go to Matthew 22:37–40 or Matthew 7:12 to make this clear. We are all guilty (Romans 3:23).

God has given us a conscience to help us feel bad when we are guilty, but our conscience doesn't always work right. Sometimes we don't feel bad even when we are guilty (for example, the child may have been happy that he got his way by being selfish), and sometimes we feel bad when we aren't guilty (the child may think the divorce is his fault). That's why it's important to use the Bible as our standard of right and wrong, not just our feelings.

You'll probably need to help these children understand that each person is responsible for their own sins, not the sins of someone else (Romans 14:12; Revelation 20:12–13). Explore this carefully, perhaps using examples to help the children grasp this concept. Here's one example:

- What does the Bible say about stealing? Is it right or wrong (Exodus 20:15)?

- If your friend goes to the store and steals a candy bar, is your friend guilty or not guilty? Why? [Guilty, because the Bible (God's standard) says we are not supposed to steal.]
- Are you guilty of stealing the candy bar? Who is guilty? Why?
- What if nobody catches your friend? Is he guilty or not guilty?
- What if your friend thinks it's funny that he didn't get caught and doesn't feel bad about stealing? Is he guilty or not guilty? Why?
- What if your friend blames you for his stealing the candy bar, because you had your own candy bar and you were mean and wouldn't share it with him? Are you guilty for stealing the candy bar? [No.] Who is guilty for stealing the candy bar? Are you guilty for anything? [Yes, for being mean.]

Help the children resolve any true guilt by turning to God in repentance. Show them that when we confess our sins (agree with God that what we did was wrong), God forgives us (1 John 1:9). You may want to look at Psalm 103 to help the child understand what forgiveness from God is like. When God forgives, he doesn't get even with us (v. 10); instead, he gives us good things (v. 5) and crowns us with love and compassion (v. 4). This is because when we trust in Jesus as our Savior, he takes the punishment we deserve instead of us receiving it. We are forgiven. God can give us good things because Jesus took the bad things in our place.

You might ask the children draw a picture of what it's like to be forgiven and a picture of what it's like not to be forgiven. Ask them which picture best represents them.

A Word to Parents

This may have been a hard chapter to read, knowing that your divorce has caused your children to struggle. If you are going through a divorce, you are probably suffering greatly yourself. You probably understand the anguish that caused David to write Psalm 55.

> It is not an enemy who taunts me—
>> I could bear that.
> It is not my foes who so arrogantly insult me—
>> I could have hidden from them.
> Instead, it is you—my equal,
>> my companion and close friend.
> What good fellowship we once enjoyed
>> as we walked together to the house of God.
>> (vv. 12–14 NLT)

The person you thought you would spend the rest of your life with has become (in some ways) your enemy. You thought you would bring up your children together, watch their first steps together, go to their soccer games together, celebrate together when they graduated from high school, and cry together when they left home to get married.

Now you're alone, and trying to parent children alone is hard. It's made harder if you're trying to do it while your own wounds are still raw. You may barely make it through work each day without bursting into tears or exploding in frustration. After eight hours, all you may want to do is go home and be left alone. You need the Lord's comfort as desperately as your children do, and you may wonder how you can possibly help them when you feel like you are about to go under yourself.

Yet if you cling to the Lord, comfort begins to flow from you to your children (2 Corinthians 1:3–5). Just as your suffering has probably made you more sensitive to what Christ suffered on your behalf, you're now able to be more sensitive and effective in comforting your children because you are also experiencing the comfort of Christ.

The apostle Paul experienced this kind of comfort when he faced "deadly perils," situations far beyond his ability to endure. Even though the dangers you face are not the same as his, they are no less perilous. Dangers such as suicidal thinking, despair, bitterness, vengeance, and hopelessness may be battling to kill your soul. But as you set your hope on God to deliver you, comfort can flow out of you to your children.

You and your children can cling to the Savior who will never leave you or forsake you. You can cling to the God who exchanged his Son's life for yours because you are precious in his sight and he loves you (Isaiah 43:4; John 3:16).

To those who have trusted in Christ as their Redeemer, God promises to be with them in deep waters and to keep the waters from drowning them. With God as your helper, you will be given the strength to guide your children rather than shut them out in an effort to escape. You will be given the strength to treat your former spouse with courtesy and consideration. You will be given the strength to encourage your children to have a good relationship with your former spouse (and his or her new mate if remarriage occurs) as well as with you. With God as your helper, you can humbly confess ways you may have sinned against your child and receive forgiveness both from God and your child.

Ways to reduce loyalty conflicts for your children

We've seen that loyalty conflicts are one of the hardest things children face after parental divorce. However, you can mitigate this for your children. Research consistently shows that parents who work to maintain a courteous relationship after a divorce greatly ease the pressure felt by their children to choose sides. Children tend to do better in all areas when their parents have a solid working relationship.

Of course, that's easier said than done. It is very tempting to want the children to side with you against the other parent. You may have been wronged, and having your children take your side may provide some vindication for that betrayal.

Additionally, you've already lost your spouse. You may fear that if your children choose to be loyal to the other parent, you will lose them too. Adding such sorrow to the grief you are already experiencing feels like it would be an insurmountable loss.

Your former spouse may be suing you in court for custody. He or she may be trying to win your children's affection by offering gifts and refusing them nothing. Your former spouse may be good at appearing likeable and innocent to everyone else, while you know from experience it is all a front.

The psalmist knew what this was like. In Psalm 55:20–21 he says,

> My companion stretched out his hand against his friends;
>> he violated his covenant.
> His speech was smooth as butter,
>> yet war was in his heart;
> his words were softer than oil,
>> yet they were drawn swords. (ESV)

What do you do in situations like this? The psalmist learned what to do and it's something you can do as well. In verse 22 he gives this solution:

Cast your burden on the LORD.

The psalmist doesn't just tell you what to do, he also tells you why. Cast your burden on the Lord *because*:

He will sustain you;
he will never permit
    the righteous to be moved.

As you cry out to God, evening, morning, and noon (see Psalm 55:17), God will give you the strength to help your children practice true biblical love toward you *and* your former spouse.

Some ways to put this into practice might include:

- Pray daily with your children, asking God to bless your former spouse and your spouse's new mate if there has been a remarriage.
- Help your children pick out cards and presents for your former spouse for birthdays and holidays.
- Save school papers your children did well on so they can share them with their other parent.
- Explain to your children that you want them to have a good relationship with your former spouse and any new family members your children might have, such as a stepparent or stepsiblings. Explain that you want your children to have the kind of love for their other family that God has for them.

- Require the children to participate in visitation (assuming they are safe) whether they want to or not. If your children feel loyal to you, they may not want to be with their other parent. Treat visitation as an expected part of life, and encourage the children to show love to their other parent (and new family members) during visitation. You may also want to foster the children's regular communication with the other parent, such as having the child call them after school.

- If possible, sit with your former spouse at events you both attend for your child.[3] Do this even if your former spouse has begun a new romantic relationship and it would require you to sit with your "replacement."

  Unquestionably, you will need to cry out to God with a fervor you may never have had before. Remember, your Savior will sustain you. He will *never* let the righteous fall. Situations like this will be hard, but God won't let them destroy you.

At this point, your future may look unendurably hard, but if you belong to the Lord, he *will* sustain you. Cling to him. He is a Savior who can bring beauty out of ashes and leave you without regrets.

CHAPTER 18
FACING DEATH AND GRIEF:
HOPE AND HELP FOR HURTING CHILDREN

BOB KELLEMEN

Nothing can shake a child's world quite like the death of a loved one. And no one can comfort a grieving child like the One who is a man of sorrows, acquainted with grief (Isaiah 53:3). Jared, who was ten, helps us picture how we can relate Christ's life-giving story to a child's encounter with death.

Jared's Terror

As Jared was walking home with a friend from a local park, he was surprised to see his mom drive up. "Get in the car, Jared. Your grandfather just passed away." Shocked by these abrupt words, Jared responded, "You're kidding," as if his mom would tease about something like this. But that's what shock does.

The next few days were a whirlwind. Grandpa's death was unexpected. This was Jared's first experience with the death of anyone close to him, and he was totally unprepared. So was the family.

They attended our church once or twice a year—on holidays—but at this point Jared's parents had not made a personal commitment to Christ. The funeral visitation was at an Eastern Orthodox Church where Jared's grandparents had been nominally involved. No one prepared Jared for what he would experience. Walking into the funeral home in his little suit and tie that his dad bought him, Jared was immediately hit with an unfamiliar odor—incense used by the Orthodox priest.

Jared was then ushered forward to the open casket. He was terrified. He'd never seen a dead body, except on TV. Grandpa was so pale. So stiff. So . . . dead. Jared's whole body reacted—he felt sick to his stomach, his palms were sweaty, his heart raced, and he thought he was going to faint. He wanted to be anywhere but there.

Then the first of several visitation services began. The Orthodox priest entered, waving an incense holder and singing—or was it chanting—in *another* language. It was all so otherworldly for Jared—creepy . . . and scary . . . and petrifying.

The funeral and burial were difficult enough, but then the more traumatic incident occurred. A week after the funeral Jared's mom, in an almost off-handed comment, said, "Last night I was in the kitchen and I thought I heard Grandpa call out my name. It was so weird."

Now to Jared's grief and confusion was added paralyzing fear. *Would Grandpa haunt me too?* he thought. That night Jared lay in bed, stiff as a board, afraid to close his eyes in the dark, wondering whether his Grandpa would appear to him.

Thus began several weeks of barely sleeping. Needing not just a night-light on, but the full room light on. Needing someone in his room until, out of exhaustion, Jared final dozed off.

Mom and Dad felt clueless to help. They first went to their family doctor, who recommended counseling and prescribed a mild sleeping pill "to take the edge off." Then Jared's parents remembered hearing about free counseling at our church and decided, "Let's call and see if they can help Jared."

Mom and Dad (Elyse and Dexter) called the church and explained their need: "Our son is not handling the death of his grandfather well at all. He can't sleep. He's terrified Grandpa is going to appear to him. We're at our wit's end." Our counseling department receptionist shared that "Pastor Bob works with a lot of families and he's even written a couple books on grief.[1] He'd be glad to meet with the two of you and Jared. With a child Jared's age, Pastor Bob typically likes to meet first with the parents so he can understand the issues. Would this be okay with the two of you?"

"As long as he meets with us *soon*, it'll be fine!"

The next day I made some points of connection with Elyse and Dexter and shared what I knew from the Initial Intake they completed. Then I asked if they could tell me more of their concerns, the history of what happened, how they had responded, how Jared was doing, and how they were doing. We also discussed what "successful" counseling would look like in their eyes—what end goal were they hoping for.

Biblical Counseling for Death and Grief: The Bible as Our Lens

I added one more piece to our conversation. Since they rarely attended church, I wanted to be sure they understood the basis for my counseling. "Dexter and Elyse, I can tell that you care about Jared and are very concerned for him. Your entire family is going through a difficult, but very normal, time of grieving. I'd be delighted to come alongside you all and offer my help." I could barely finish those words before they were thanking me effusively.

Then I continued, "You guys laughed a little sheepishly when you said, 'We don't come here very often.' Since you may not know exactly how we do things around here, I want to be sure we're all on the same page about what to expect. You can tell from our first hour together that I'm not going to 'beat you over the head with the Bible.' However, (I held my Bible at my eye level), I will seek to have all of my counsel come from a biblical worldview. The Bible will be my lens for helping Jared—and you—think through how to handle death and grief. Because for me, there is no way to find hope as we face death and no way to find healing as we deal with grief other than through God's Word and God's Son." Having agreed to this focus, we made plans for Dexter and Elyse to bring Jared in to see me the next day.

The Journey of Grief

In counseling children struggling with death and grief, I use a modified version of a grief journey model outlined in *God's Healing for Life's Losses*. In it, I seek to help children and their parents move from the typical *natural* response to death, to a *supernatural* response to death by facing loss face-to-face with Christ.

The Grief Journey: Facing Loss Face-to-Face with Christ

Typical Human Grief Response	Biblical Redeemed Grief Response
Denial/Isolation	Candor: Honesty with Yourself
Anger/Resentment	Complaint/Lament: Honesty with God
Bargaining/Works	Cry Out to God: Asking God for Help
Depression/Alienation	Comfort: Receiving God's Help[2]

Journey Marker #1: Helping children move from pretending to honesty

When Jared's parents told him they were taking him to a counselor, he was upset. "Who is he? Why am I going?" When they told Jared my name, his eyes lit up. "I know him! He's the Pastor dude that's also a wrestling coach. He coached me at camp last summer. I like him!"

Jared and his parents decided that after a brief time (five minutes) when we were all in my office, I would meet with Jared alone, and then his parents would return for our last fifteen minutes. After hearing how Jared's wrestling season was going, we shifted focus. "I understand from Mom and Dad that the whole family is having a hard time with the loss of your grandfather. I think you called him 'Grandpa,' right?"

After Jared shared a bit, I sensed he felt embarrassed that he—a wrestler—was so fearful. So I shared some of my past struggles with fears related to death. "Even tough-guy wrestlers like us can be afraid. Death is a big opponent."

I then explained to Jared that one of the ways people try to deal with death, loss, and fear is to pretend—to deny that it happened. I mentioned casually that his response to his mom— "You're kidding"—is one common form of denial or pretending. To help Jared picture the problem with denial, I asked if he ever tried to keep a beach ball below the water when his family was on their annual Florida beach vacation. He laughed. "Oh yeah! It always squirms up and pops waaay into the air!"

"Denial or pretending is like that, Jared. We try not to face the pain of losing Grandpa, but it comes up somewhere. I wonder if part of where it's coming up is in your fears at night. Did you know that the Bible talks about moving from pretending to being honest?" We then read Psalm 42:5 (NIV) together. "Why, my soul, are you downcast? Why so disturbed within me?"

270

"David was a tough guy. A king. A warrior. But he felt sad and anxious, depressed and fearful. Instead of pretending, he was honest with himself. Instead of letting his emotions talk to him, *David talked back to his emotions.* Do you think you and I could do that? I'll go first if you want. I'll share some of the fears and sadness I've had when I've lost loved ones. Then you can go next."

So, we shared stories—fear stories and sadness stories. What started in this first meeting, continued for a couple meetings, including in-between meetings as I asked Jared to write down additional fear and sadness stories and show them to me each week.

Journey Marker #2: Helping children move from anger to lamenting to God—our big and loving Shepherd-King

As Jared and I continued journeying together, I mentioned that a lot of people, once they quit pretending, end up admitting how angry they were—that their loved one died and that God allowed this to happen. I said, "A lot of people end up shaking their fists at God, seeing him like an unfair wrestling referee."

Jared reminded me that he had attended Vacation Bible School at our church "when I was just a kid—nine. I asked Jesus to be my Savior. But I don't think Mom and Dad have done that yet." We talked further about this, and I sensed that Jared truly knew Jesus.

"So, Jared, could we talk again about Warrior-King David and how he talked to God? David not only talked to his own soul—like we saw in Psalm 42:5— David talked *to God.* When he was upset, he lamented. He told God whatever was in his heart. He knew that God knew everything he

271

was thinking anyway. David knew that God was big enough to handle whatever he felt so he shared his heart with God. People can do that when they have a biblical picture of God as both *big* and *loving*." So we explored a picture of God from Isaiah 40:10–11.

> See, the Sovereign LORD comes with power, and he rules with a mighty arm. See, his reward is with him, and his recompense accompanies him. He tends his flock like a shepherd: He gathers the lambs in his arms and carries them close to his heart; he gently leads those that have young. (NIV)

We talked about how verse 10 pictures God as a big/strong King and how verse 11 pictures God as a loving/caring Shepherd. Understanding that God is both *big* and *loving* opened Jared up to lamenting—sharing his fears, sadness, and madness with God.

Together we read Psalm 13 and Psalm 88 as two examples of God's people doing just that. Over several meetings and in-between meetings, Jared was able to give voice to emotions—this time not just to himself, but also to his *big* and *loving* Savior—to his Shepherd-King.

Journey Marker #3: Helping children move from depending on myself to crying out to God—who hears and cares, delivers and saves

Elyse and Dexter were reporting that good things were happening with Jared. He seemed more at peace. Less fearful. But his night terrors and sleep anxieties were still there.

As Jared and I continued on our trek together, I explained another typical stage as people try to handle their grief when

272

a loved one dies. "They try to manipulate or con God." Jared thought that was ridiculous! "God's too strong to be man . . . manip . . . how do you say it? And he's too smart to be conned!" I gave the example of a father who might bargain with God, "I'll quit drinking if you'll cure my daughter of leukemia." I mentioned that we try to use God like Aladdin's genie in a bottle.

Then we discussed what to do instead of that. "We cry out to God in humble dependence. While God won't be manipulated, he does love to rescue us when we humbly cry out to him." Jared and his parents had recently seen the school play *Oliver* where young Oliver meekly and respectfully asks the master of the orphanage, "Please, sir, may I have some more." I mentioned, "That should be our posture toward our Shepherd-King: arms held up with an empty bowl, pleading for more, asking humbly for help." We then read together Psalm 34:17–18.

> The righteous cry out, and the LORD hears them; he delivers them from all their troubles. The LORD is close to the brokenhearted and saves those who are crushed in spirit. (NIV)

After talking through what Jared was afraid of at night—what he thought would happen if Grandpa appeared to him—we then brought biblical truth to bear on those fears. And we applied biblical images of God to those fears. When his night terrors struck, Jared began to cry out in prayer to the Lord who was not only his Shepherd-King, but also, to use Jared's hyphenated phrase, "God-Who-Hears-and-Cares-Delivers-and-Saves!"

Journey Marker #4: Helping children move from depression to comfort in Christ—our comforting and encouraging divine Counselor

I cautioned Jared that as he dealt with his fears, he might end up having to deal more with his sadness. "It's like winning the first round of a wrestling tourney, and then turning around and having to face the next guy who is even tougher. Your fears may even be one way of not having to fully face the fact that Grandpa is gone."

Now I "leveraged" my good relationship with Jared to point him to the Better Counselor, the Best Counselor, the Divine Counselor. "Jared, it's meant a lot to me that you've expressed how much I've helped you. But, I'm human. I can't always be there with you. But there is One who will never leave or forsake you. He will always be with you. He will always be *in* you!"

We then read together John 14 and the promise that Jesus would send another Counselor to be *in* us forever, never leaving us as orphans (vv. 15–18). I could tell how much it helped Jared to know that though Grandpa had left him, Jesus *never* would.

Then we pictured two meanings of this word for the Spirit as our Counselor. "Jared, first this word *Counselor* means Comforter." I wrote on the whiteboard, *Co-Fortitude.* "The Spirit is in you to fortify you, to strengthen you. Jared, right when you feel those night terrors, how would it help you to picture the Spirit as your Fort or Fortress surrounding you and protecting you?"

After interacting about this, I wrote a second word on the white board, *En-Courage.* "Jared, the Spirit is also in you as your Encourager—to place God's courage in you. When you are facing those sleep anxieties and fears, how could you

274

tap into the Spirit as your En-Courager giving you courage to face your fears?"

Little by little, Jared has found victory *in* his fears and hope *in* his sadness and loss. The fears did not magically disappear, but Jesus's presence gave Jared the courage to face his fears. Jared's sadness did not—and should not have—disappeared, but Jesus's comfort brought healing hope to Jared's tender heart.

A Word to Parents: Three Phrases for Parents

Parents, I've always believed that kids need good parenting more than they need good counseling. Parents can be their kids' best biblical counselors. With those truths in mind, here are three phrases for parental biblical counselors of their own children.

Parental Reminder #1: It's helpful to prepare

As you likely picked up in Jared's vignette, his parents could have prepared him better for what he was about to face. It's understandable that they did not—they were not prepared either. Nothing truly prepares us for death. But a few actions and attitudes can help.

Pray before communicating. Elyse blurting out, "Get in the car, Jared. Your Grandfather just passed away," could have been improved with a prayer, *Father, help me to communicate this difficult loss in the gentlest way possible.*

Communicate before attending funeral services. Jared was ill-prepared for the incense, the chanting, and the open casket. Walk your children through what they are likely to experience. Talk openly with them about their questions.

Parental Reminder #2: It's normal to feel

Jared felt a variety of emotions: grief, sadness, fear, and anger. Death is an intruder. It has a piercing stinger that wounds deeply.

Allow your children to lament. Don't force them to "get it together."

Give your children permission to grieve. One of the most powerful ways to do this is by giving yourself permission to grieve and allowing your children to experience—to the degree they can handle it—your own sadness.

Mourn with your children when they mourn. Hurt with them when they hurt. As you lament to God, you receive comfort from the Father of compassion and the God of all comfort. And then the comfort you receive from Christ spills over from Christ to you to your child (2 Corinthians 1:3–5).

Realize that for children's actions often express emotions. Children rarely have the emotional intelligence or maturity to verbalize exactly what they feel. Their actions speak for their emotions. Seek to prayerfully discern what emotional message your child's behavior is sending.

Parental Reminder #3: It's possible to hope

While death has its sting, we also have 1 Corinthians 15:54–47:

> "Death has been swallowed up in victory." Where, O death, is your victory? Where, O death, is your sting? The sting of death is sin, and the power of sin is the law. But thanks be to God! He gives us the victory through our Lord Jesus Christ. (NIV)

You not only give your children permission to grieve, you also offer them encouragement to cling to Christ. Model for them your clinging-courage as you take your grief to Christ your Victor, to Christ your big and loving Shepherd-King, to Christ your Deliverer and Savior, to Christ who hears and cares, to Christ your comforting and encouraging Divine Counselor.

Bathe your children in hope-giving Scripture. Death is when the Word comes alive—what a paradox. The written Word points to Christ the Living Word—who is alive forevermore. Read Scripture together. Weep Scripture together. Cling to Scripture together. Pray Scripture together.

Relate God's story to your child's story. Picture it like this: You stand with your children between two worlds, between two stories—the earthly temporal story of death and the heavenly eternal story of life. With one foot, always pivot into your child's earthly story of grief, pain, hurt, loss, and confused feelings. With the other foot, always pivot together with your child into Christ's heavenly, hope-filled story.

Remind your children that you've read the end of the story. Life triumphs over death, hope triumphs over hurt, and Christ triumphs over the devil and evil.

> And I heard a loud voice from the throne saying, "Look! God's dwelling place is now among the people, and he will dwell with them. They will be his people, and God himself will be with them and be their God. 'He will wipe every tear from their eyes. There will be no more death' or mourning or crying or pain, for the old order of things has passed away." (Revelation 21:3–4 NIV)

CHAPTER 19
COUNSELING CHILDREN NOT LIVING WITH THEIR BIOLOGICAL PARENTS

PAM BAUER

Nine-year-old Elena is currently in her third living situation. She was born in Russia and lived with her biological family for four years. Surviving for the family was a daily challenge. When Elena's mother had a baby boy, Elena helped take care of him. But then Elena's father lost his job. Often, Elena went to bed hungry, crying herself to sleep. In the mornings, she would beg her mother for food, but there was none. The family was desperate.

Eventually, Elena's father took her on a trip to an orphanage in the neighboring village. While Elena did not understand the purpose of an orphanage, she enjoyed watching the children play. She was happy when they invited her to have milk with them. Her father left without a word and never came back.

For months, Elena waited for her father to come and get her. It became more than her young heart could bear. She descended into grief, anger, despair, hopelessness, and finally became numb. She cried herself to sleep at night until she couldn't cry anymore. She blamed herself. If only she hadn't begged her mother for extra food. If only she hadn't wanted the cup of milk.

Elena stayed in the orphanage for two years. She attended school and attempted to learn, but it was hard to think while she missed her mother so much. The older children picked on her. She learned to be invisible to avoid unwanted attention.

When Elena turned six, an orphanage worker told her that her mother would come the following day to adopt her and take her to America. Elena was thrilled! Finally, her mother had found her. But the next day, instead of her mother, a strange woman and her husband came. Everyone exclaimed that these were her new parents. But Elena already had a mother and father. She did not want a new family. She wanted her family. This was confusing.

The new people removed her from the orphanage, put her in new clothing, and spoke in a foreign language. They flew on an airplane together to America, and soon she arrived at their home—a completely unfamiliar house. Nothing was normal. Elena desperately wanted her biological mother. Would her mother be able to find her now? Everyone acted as if Elena should be happy, but Elena was confused, desperate, and frightened.

Elena struggled to adapt to her adoptive family. She began wetting the bed and having bad dreams. She didn't understand what anyone was saying. It was hard to remember to put her toys away and follow other household rules. Everything was different. There was plenty of food, but nothing familiar. Sometimes Elena would steal food or eat too much too fast in an attempt to drive away her aching emptiness.

Over time, Elena realized people in her new home expected her to be their child. She demonstrated in many ways she was not their daughter. She didn't choose these people. She would not submit to them. Elena did not let herself need this family. She rebelled, lied, manipulated, and stole. When she didn't get her way, Elena would scream, yell, kick, and bite. She just wanted these people to leave her alone. When confronted about her misbehavior, Elena showed no remorse or guilt.

At school Elena struggled to concentrate during class. She wasn't interested in learning or getting to know the other children or teachers. She only cared about herself. She wanted to do what she wanted to do.

Everywhere Elena went, she talked to strangers to see if anyone knew her mother.

Her adoptive parents, Rick and Sarah, have come for help. They love Elena, but she doesn't respond well to them. Is she even capable of love? Nothing they do seems to reach her heart. Her behavior is getting worse, and her parents are concerned about the coming teen years with a child so out of control. The gulf between them and her appears to be widening. They are at a loss as to what to do.

In Elena's experience, relationships hurt. Her solution is to shun all relationships. She wants to leave home and live alone. She doesn't trust anyone. In her childish understanding, she believes that she can take care of herself and she plans to leave home when she is twelve.

Abandoned Children Live with Loss

Adoption is based on loss. To help an abandoned child— whether currently fostered, adopted, or living with relatives— we must look at their whole life story, not just the fact of their adoption or current placement. Elena began life with her biological parents and was subsequently abandoned. Those charged with loving her, providing for her, protecting her, and teaching her walked away when she was a vulnerable child. She was then warehoused in an orphanage with strangers tending her. Finally, she was adopted by another group of strangers. In this light, we realize that adoption is not the hope-filled story for Elena that it is for her adoptive parents.

Even children adopted as infants can experience loss and grief when they realize what adoption means. Initially, they may accept the information without an adverse effect, only to experience delayed grief at a time when they understand the concept of family better. Abandoned children suffer in many ways. They may swing through grief, anxiety, and depression. Many express their feelings by resisting the adults who are loving them or even by sabotaging the relationship. Some children are hyper-vigilant and self-reliant in anticipation of further abandonment. Others are clingy, fearful, or disengaged.

While there are many expressions of their suffering, the problem lies in their hearts. The overarching themes of their sorrow are confusion, grief, and fear. With the increase in adoption, foster care, and grandparents as parents, it is likely that you will counsel children who are not biologically related to their caregivers or who live with extended family and not their parents. God's Word offers help and hope for these children and the adults who love and care for them.

Confusion

Before a child is adopted or fostered, they are abandoned. Abandonment is disorienting. The child's confusion is evident in their lack of orderly thought. They lack sequencing and cause and effect thinking, have partial information, and blame the wrong people for their troubles. They draw strange conclusions and then live emotionally instead of logically.

For example, they don't understand what has happened or why—they don't know who is responsible, or whom to trust. Often, children blame themselves or their adoptive parents for their abandonment. We can help by bringing order to their chaos.

One way to address this chaos is by helping them understand their life story in the context of God's faithfulness. Although they don't see this or feel it at this moment, the truth is that they have a faithful heavenly Father who cares (Psalm 27:10). Let the child tell their story. Ask questions to draw out events and details as well as the child's feelings and questions. As with anyone we counsel, we want to understand their story and how it impacts them.

You can help a child by taking the facts and organizing them sequentially. One way to do this is to work with the child to create a time line. For example, you might use a large roll of paper. Unroll it for five or six feet. Draw a line down the middle (lengthwise). On the upper half, record the child's life from their point of view. Mark off segments in the line to represent time frames and record life events in their appropriate location. Help them understand the sequence of events, even if the reasons are unclear. Ask if there are good memories to record and do so. In the lower half, draw the "everlasting arms" (Deuteronomy 33:27) of God. The unrolled portion of the paper represents the future and all its possibilities.

The Scripture repeatedly speaks of God's faithfulness. He will never forsake his children. He is always steadfast. The following verses speak of God's faithfulness to never forsake his children:

- It is the LORD who goes before you. He will be with you; he will not leave you or forsake you. Do not fear or be dismayed. (Deuteronomy 31:8)

- And I will dwell among the children of Israel and will not forsake my people Israel. (1 Kings 6:13)
- For the LORD will not forsake his people; he will not abandon his heritage. (Psalm 94:14)
- Can a woman forget her nursing child, that she should have no compassion on the son of her womb? Even these may forget, yet I will not forget you. Behold, I have engraved you on the palms of my hands; your walls are continually before me. (Isaiah 49:15–16)
- For he has said, "I will never leave you nor forsake you." (Hebrews 13:5)

To forsake is to abandon, desert, or leave behind. This is the experience of the abandoned child. But God promises to never leave. God remains faithful, even when biological parents are not. He continues to watch over the orphan. The adoptive parents are God's mercy to the child. While adoptive parents never replace birth parents, they provide protection, love, nurture, and a family that a child can eventually love.

Scripture brings great comfort to the heart of a child who has felt lost and been tossed aside. Help them remember times when they experienced God's faithfulness and add it to the time line. Psalm 139 would be another source of comfort. A child may feel disposable, but God's Word proclaims that he knows each person intimately and cares deeply. He will never abandon his children. Keep bringing the child back to God's faithfulness and mercy. God can be trusted.

Frequently, a child will blame the adoptive parents for their situation. The child believes their biological parents were returning, and the adoptive parents interrupted the reunion. This thinking sets the child against the adoptive parents.

Knowing whatever truth is available—who did what and when—helps the child to think correctly about their adoptive parents as people who love them and want to help.

Elena can come to recognize God's faithfulness. God knew her need for protection and a family. He kept her alive when she had no other resources. What a comfort to know that when she felt invisible and worthless the God of heaven saw her and moved to bring her help.

Grief

Grief is another significant theme that runs through the life of an abandoned child. Adoption does not replace a biological family. There is first a significant loss. Children must be helped to grieve. Depending on the situation, biological parents may return sporadically, bringing more confusion and complicating the grief process.

"Grief is the internal response and mourning is the external response to loss."[1] By the time adoption or foster placement occurs, months or years may have passed since the initial separation of the child from their biological parents. Children are no longer crying or asking about their birth family. They have given up hope of ever seeing them. With the absence of tears, adoptive parents do not realize their children are grieving and needing help.

Abandoned children are among the "brokenhearted" people referred to in Scripture. God draws near to the brokenhearted, providing rest (Matthew 11:28), and strength (Psalm 73:26), and help (Isaiah 41:10). He is compassionate and tender (James 5:11). Model the heart of God as you talk with the child.

Abandoned children benefit from permission to talk about their biological parents without feeling disloyal to their adoptive/foster parents. They need to know grief is a normal part of life in a fallen world. Reassure the child that they can grieve, cry, feel sad, and talk to their parents about their birth family. They will receive comfort from their adoptive parents. The child's life will span two families. One gives them life and the other helps them to live.

Help them to see that God is not only faithful as mentioned above, but also merciful and willing to come to their aid.

- For my father and my mother have forsaken me, but the LORD will take me in. (Psalm 27:10)
- Humble yourselves, therefore, under the mighty hand of God so that at the proper time he may exalt you, casting all your anxieties on him, because he cares for you. (1 Peter 5:6–7)

God is the God of all comfort (2 Corinthians 1:3). Children can open their hearts and talk with him about their sorrow. He will not judge or reject them for their grief. Although grief feels unbearable, Elena *can* experience the comfort of the Lord. He understands her pain. He comforts her with his presence as well as the gift of a new family, who will love her and help her and hold her during her sorrow.

Fear

The third theme in adoption is fear. Fear can mean to be afraid, to perceive a threat, or be uneasy. The result is an absence of trust. It is an oppositional posture—me against you.

The hearts of abandoned children are controlled by their fear. Their goal is safety from the pain of abandonment. From the child's perspective, neither adults nor God have made good decisions for their lives. Therefore, they do not trust adults or God—they trust themselves, desiring to protect their hearts from further pain. Some are overly clingy, fearing re-abandonment and seeking to control their circumstances as protection. Others use rage to keep everyone at a safe distance to avoid potential pain. Learning to love threatens their self-made protective fortress.

But Scripture presents another kind of fear. It is the fear of the Lord. This is a reverence of God that recognizes his exalted position and his goodness. It leads to trusting and drawing near to him because of his mercy. It draws a person under the protection and provision from the Lord—a state of blessedness. The resulting posture is submission and dependence.

The psalmist states the following:

- Oh, fear the LORD, you his saints, for those who fear him have no lack! (Psalm 34:9)
- Come, O children, listen to me; I will teach you the fear of the LORD. (Psalm 34:11)
- The angel of the LORD encamps around those who fear him, and delivers them. (Psalm 34:7)

Terrifying fear is the right response to God for anyone who is not born of the Spirit of God. And holy fear is the right response of every person who belongs to God. The abandoned child needs to learn the gospel and the fear of the Lord. God is the answer to every good desire of the abandoned child's heart—a Father who is always there, always provides, always protects. Share the gospel. Even young children can comprehend the Good News. A child's heart is fertile ground for redemption.

There is a parallel here. The adopted child needs to respond to God's invitation to enter his family. Likewise, they must respond to the invitation of an adoptive family. Adoption is a legal status that happens to a child. It is also a relationship that both parents and the adopted child must enter willingly. As a counselor, you can help the child understand that they must choose.

For example, talk about different kinds of love. Discuss the things and people that the child does love, perhaps birth parents, siblings, a special friend, the family dog. Talk about how each love feels to them. God brings many people into our lives for us to love, and he never tells us to stop loving them. The child can love their biological parents and their adoptive parents. We don't have to love everyone the same. Ask them, "Will you agree to let God make room in your heart for the love of your adoptive parents, too?"

Over time, Elena can learn to overcome her fear and begin to trust again. She can understand and experience God's faithfulness, his comfort, and his goodness. He is worthy of her trust. The psalmist states, "God sets the lonely in families." It is his gift because he is good.

A Word to Parents

Adoption is not easy for the child or the parent. Remember, your perspectives are different. As parents, you want to move forward to becoming a loving family together. But the child is still dealing with the past. It takes time for children to learn to love and trust again and then enter a relationship with you as a son or daughter. Be patient. It will take much longer than you expect for your child to trust you. In the long view, adoption is a blessing to them. But for now, it signifies the loss of their biological family.

Question your child gently and often. Do not assume you understand what they mean. For example, when you see strange behavior, ask, "Where did you learn this?" or "Who taught you this?" instead of jumping in to correct behavior. If you do correct them, and they cover their head and curl into a ball, don't start with "I won't hit you." Get down on the floor and gently ask, "Who taught you to be afraid of adults?" In their pain, children are vulnerable. They might allow you to truly comfort them or they may not, but you can always offer comfort. Speak healing words. Remind them that they are precious. Share in their sorrow over their suffering. Speak words of hope.

Confusion, grief, or fear won't look the way you expect. Abandoned children have learned to hide their feelings. Again, ask. For example, a child looking at the floor when being disciplined might be sorry, or he might be hiding his anger. A child who is scared often looks you right in the eyes to see if you are a threat. As a parent, you might misinterpret this eye contact as trust instead of what it really is—fear. Ask, "What are you wanting?"

Assume most misbehavior stems from confusion, grief, or fear. Ask questions. Even angry behavior is often based on fear. Explain the truth of a situation. Address the heart issues. Then help the child to respond with correct behavior. Let them rehearse correct responses and give reassuring feedback.

Abandonment is devastating to a child, but it is not a hopeless situation. It may produce fertile soil for eternal redemption. In God's mercy, he has provided second chance homes for many of such children.

It took time for Elena to realize that her life is different from what she thought it would be, but it is still good.

She does have a second family, an adoptive family who loves her and treasures her. She still gets angry and overwhelmed at times, but her mother always reminds her of the truth—Elena is her precious daughter. She is learning to trust God and her parents to help her find the answers to her questions through God's faithful Word.

Endnotes

Chapter 1

1. The names and stories of the children mentioned in this book have been altered to protect their identities.

2. Joe Thorn, "Praying for Your Pastor," *Joe Thorn* (blog), September 18, 2012, http://www.joethorn.net/blog/2012/09/18/praying-for-your-pastor.

Chapter 2

1. See chapter 3, Julie Lowe, "Counseling Children of Different Age Groups," for additional help in this area.

2. Donna A. Henderson and Charles L. Thompson, *Counseling Children*, 8th Edition (Belmont, CA: Brooks/Cole Cengage Learning, 2011), 88.

3. John Piper, "Your Executioner May Laugh You to Scorn for Quoting Psalm 91," *Desiring God* (article), August 15, 2002. https://www.desiringgod.org/articles/your-executioner-may-laugh-you-to-scorn-for-quoting-psalm-91. John Piper unpacks this passage with this helpful summary: I conclude that Psalm 91 means two things about the suffering of the saints. One is that often God amazingly delivers them physically when others around them are falling. The other is that God often wills for his children to suffer, but forbids that the suffering hurts them in the end. Such evil will never befall you.

Chapter 3

1. Chapter adapted from Julie Lowe, *Building Bridges: Biblical Counseling Activities for Children and Teens* (Greensboro, NC: New Growth Press, 2020). Used by permission.

2. See Julie Lowe's latest book, *Building Bridges: Biblical Counseling Activities for Children and Teens* (Greensboro, NC: New Growth Press,

2020), for additional examples of biblical counseling activities for children of different ages.

Chapter 4

1. Adapted by Marty Machowski from his minibook, *Leading Your Child to Christ: Biblical Direction for Sharing the Gospel* (Greensboro, NC: New Growth Press, 2012).

2. Charles Spurgeon, *Spiritual Parenting* (New Kensington, PA: Whitaker House, 2003), 58.

3. Wayne Grudem, *Bible Doctrine*, ed. Jeff Purswell (Grand Rapids: Zondervan Publishing House, 1999), 297.

4. *Bible Doctrine*, 312.

Chapter 6

1. For further reading, see Tim Keeter's, *Help! My Child Is Being Bullied* (Wapwallopen, PA: Shepherd Press, 2019).

Chapter 7

1. Adapted by Julie Lowe from her minibook, *Helping Your Anxious Child: What to Do When Worries Get Big* (Greensboro, NC: New Growth Press, 2018).

2. Paul Foxman, *The Worried Child: Recognizing Anxiety in Children and Helping Them Heal* (Alameda, CA: Hunter House Publishers, 2004), 2.

3. This activity is taken from Julie Lowe, *Building Bridges: Biblical Counseling Activities for Children and Teens* (Greensboro, NC: New Growth Press, 2020). It also includes other activities that you can use to help children identify their fears and take to God for comfort and help.

Chapter 8

1. Adapted by Michael R. Emlet from his minibook *Angry Children: Understanding and Helping Your Child Regain Control* (Greensboro, NC: New Growth Press, 2008).

2. I am indebted to David Powlison for this way of describing the relationship between the heart and physical/situational factors in the life of a child.

3. List adapted from Ross W. Green and J. Stuart Ablon, *Treating Explosive Kids: The Collaborative Problem-Solving Approach* (New York: Guilford Press, 2006), 18.

4. See Scott Turansky and Joanne Miller, *Good and Angry: Exchanging Frustration for Character . . . In You and Your Kids* (Colorado Springs, CO: Shaw Books, 2002), 67–69.

Chapter 9

1. Suicide Datasheet, CDC, https://www.cdc.gov/violenceprevention/pdf/suicide-datasheet-a.pdf. Suicide is the third leading cause of death for 15- to 24-year-old Americans. Females are more likely than males to have had suicidal thoughts, and females attempt suicide three times as often as males.

2. One such tool is the Suicide Assessment Five-Step Evaluation and Triage (SAFE-T), http://www.sprc.org.

3. For further information on suicide prevention, the following websites offer helpful guidance: http://suicideprevention.nv.gov/Youth/Myths/, https://www.verywellmind.com/common-myths-about-teen-suicide-2611327, https://www.nami.org/Blogs/NAMI-Blog/September-2018/5-Common-Myths-About-Suicide-Debunked.

Chapter 10

1. Adapted by Edward T. Welch from his minibook, *Helping Children with Shame: Resting in God's Approval* (Greensboro, NC: New Growth Press, 2020).

Chapter 12

1. A much more developed discussion of these concepts from a biblical perspective may be found in David White, *God, You, and Sex: A Profound Mystery* (Greensboro, NC: New Growth Press, 2019). An abridged version of that discussion may be found in Tim Geiger, *Explaining LGBTQ+ Identity to Your Child* (Greensboro, NC: New Growth Press, 2018).

2. Married spouses are always identified in the larger context of Scripture as one man and one woman, in an exclusive, lifelong covenant (see Genesis 2:18–24; Matthew 19:4–6).

3. This point is critical. The majority of non-biblical sexual desire (i.e., sinful lust) and behavior is motivated by a selfish desire to serve oneself instead of serving one's spouse. Lust, sexual behavior, and LGBTQ+ sexual identification among children are often tied to using sex, gender, or the attitudes and emotions associated with them to achieve self-perceptions of happiness, connectedness, safety, and control by themselves. This is a subjective, self-serving use of sex and gender.

4. Not only do we never see a case of a person's gender diverging from his or her birth sex anywhere in Scripture, but all individuals seen or spoken of in post-death/resurrected sense maintain congruity between their birth sex and present gender. Some examples include Moses and Elijah (Mark 9:2–8); the rich man, Lazarus, and Abraham (Luke 16:19–31); Jesus (John 20:11–21:23 and Revelation 1:12–18).

5. Author and counselor Paul Tripp provides a superb explanation of these disordered desires in his book *Instruments in the Redeemer's Hands* (Phillipsburg, NJ: P&R Publishing, 2002), 75–94.

6. Mary Jo Ridley, "Pick Your Pain: Facing Your Fears About the Talk," *Harvest USA* blog, https://www.harvestusa.org/pick-your-pain-facing-your-fears-about-the-talk/#.Xa31bkZKjD4. This article is a free resource by the founder and president of The Birds & The Bees, and organization with many additional resources to help parents.

7. Some recommended resources are: David White, *God, You, and Sex: A Profound Mystery (Greensboro, NC: New Growth Press, 2019)*; Harvest USA, *Alive: Gospel Sexuality for Students* (Greensboro, NC: New Growth Press, 2018); and Tim Geiger, *Explaining LGBTQ+ Identity to Your Child* (Greensboro, NC: New Growth Press, 2018). Additionally, many other resources, for sale or free, are available at the Harvest USA website, https://harvestusa.org.

Chapter 13

1. Catherine Glen, PhD, Matthew K Nook, PhD, "Nonsuicidal self-injury in children and adolescents: Clinical features and proposed diagnostic criteria." Uptodate.com, July 16, 2019. Retrieved electronically.

2. Catherine Glen, PhD, Matthew K Nook, PhD, "Nonsuicidal self-injury in children and adolescents: Epidemiology and risk factors." Uptodate.com, July 16, 2019. Retrieved electronically.

Chapter 14

1. Excerpted from Rachel O'Neil's post on Make September Gold-Childhood Cancer Awareness, Facebook, September 20, 2018, https://www.facebook.com/MakeSeptemberGold/photos/a.57339609 6030424/1827332190636802/?type=3&theater.

2. Colin Mattoon, "Counseling the Chronically Ill," *Biblical Counseling Coalition*, May 1, 2013, https://www.biblicalcounselingcoalition.org/2013/05/01/counseling-the-chronically-ill/.

3. Colin Mattoon, "A Guide to Counseling the Chronically Ill," *Biblical Counseling Coalition*, May 1, 2013, https://www.biblicalcounselingcoalition.org/wp-content/uploads/2013/05/mattoon_a_guide_to_counseling_the_chronically_ill.pdf, p. 6.

4. "From Wrestling to Finding Rest," *Joni and Friends*, July 17, 2019, https://www.joniandfriends.org/from-wrestling-to-finding-rest/.

5. "From Wrestling to Finding Rest."

6. "Leading Through Brokenness," *Joni and Friends*, July 18, 2019, https://youtu.be/-tEcJFigJjg.

7. Jeff Robinson, "5 Ways to Talk to Your Children About Death," *The Gospel Coalition*, September 14, 2015, https://www.thegospelcoalition.org/article/5-ways-talk-to-your-children-about-death/.

8. Joni Eareckson Tada, "God's Parent Support Group," *Joni and Friends Radio*, Sept. 12, 2017, https://www.joniandfriends.org/gods-parent-support-group/.

9. Rick Vacek, "Tada Delivers a Moving Call to Action at Chapel," *GCU Today*, September 18, 2018, https://news.gcu.edu/2018/09/tada-delivers-a-moving-call-to-action-at-chapel/.

10. Costi W. Hinn "Trusting Christ with Childhood Cancer," *For The Gospel*, February 18, 2019, http://www.forthegospel.org/trusting-christ-with-childhood-cancer/.

11. Amy E. Mason, *Bible Promises for Parents of Children with Special Needs* (Carol Stream, IL: Tyndale House Publishers, 2017), 147.

Chapter 15

1. "What Is Autism?" *Autism Speaks*, https://www.autismspeaks.org/what-autism.

2. Mark Shaw, "Continuing the Conversation on a Biblical Understanding of Autism," *Biblical Counseling Coalition*, March 18, 2019, https://www.biblicalcounselingcoalition.org/2019/03/18/continuing-the-conversation-on-a-biblical-understanding-of-autism/#_ftn1.

3. "Continuing the Conversation on a Biblical Understanding of Autism."

4. Joni Eareckson Tada and Steve Bundy, with Pat Verbal, *Beyond Suffering for the Next Generation Study Guide* (Agoura Hills, CA: Joni and Friends, 2015).

5. Boris Vujicic, *Raising the Perfectly Imperfect Child: Facing Challenges with Strength, Courage, and Hope* (Colorado Springs, CO: WaterBrook Press, 2016), 11.

6. Joni Eareckson Tada, "Tough Questions . . . Tender Answers," *Joni and Friends* blog, October 13, 2011, https://www.joniandfriends.org/tough-questions-tender-answers/.

7. Lilly Park, "Theology of the Soul as It Relates to Disability," *Biblical Counseling Coalition*, January 17, 2018, https://www.biblicalcounselingcoalition.org/2018/01/17/bcc-summit-2017-theology-of-the-soul-as-it-relates-to-disability/.

8. Amy E. Mason, *Bible Promises for Parents of Children with Special Needs* (Carol Stream, IL: Tyndale House Publishers, 2017), 120–122.

9. Joni and Friends, *Real Families, Real Needs* (Carol Stream, IL: Tyndale House Publishers, 2017), x.

10. Boris Vujicic, *Raising the Perfectly Imperfect Child: Facing Challenges with Strength, Courage, and Hope* (Colorado Springs, CO: WaterBrook Press, 2016), 4–5.

Chapter 16

1. Steve Viars, "The Presence of Bitter Conditions," June 2, 2019, sermon, Faith Church, Lafayette, IN, https://www.faithlafayette.org/resources/sermons/the-presence-of-bitter-conditions.

Chapter 17

1. Susan Arnsberg Diamond, *Helping Children of Divorce: A Handbook for Parents and Teachers* (New York: Shocken Books, 1985) as cited in Diane Medved, *The Case against Divorce* (New York: Ivy Books, 1989), 237.

2. Patricia Papernow, *Becoming a Stepfamily* (San Francisco: Jossey-Bass Publishers, 1993), 111.

3. Obviously, some former spouses won't be willing to cooperate with you in this.

Chapter 18

1. Robert Kellemen, *God's Healing for Life's Losses: How to Find Hope When You're Hurting* (Winona Lake, IN: BMH Books, 2010). See also Bob Kellemen, *Grief: Walking with Jesus* (Phillipsburg, NJ: P&R Publishing, 2018).

2. *God's Healing for Life's Losses*, 10.

Chapter 19

1. Kate Jackson, "How Children Grieve: Persistent Myths May Stand in the Way of Appropriate Care and Support for Children," *Social Work Today* 15, no. 20 (March/April 2015), https://www.socialworktoday.com/archive/030415p20.shtml.